AT THE CROSS
Big deals outside the city

At the cross
Big deals outside the city

John Benton

EP Books
Faverdale North, Darlington, DL3 0PH, England
e-mail: sales@epbooks.org
web: www.epbooks.org

EP Books USA
P. O. Box 614, Carlisle, PA 17013, USA
e-mail: usasales@epbooks.org
web: www.epbooks.us

© John Benton 2011

All rights reserved. No part of this publication may be reproduced, stored in a retrieval system or transmitted, in any form, or by any means, electronic, mechanical, photocopying, recording or otherwise, without the prior permission of the publishers.

First published 2011

British Library Cataloguing in Publication Data available

ISBN-13 978 085234 741 6   ISBN 0 85234 741 3

Unless otherwise indicated, Scripture quotations are taken from the Holy Bible, New International Version. Copyright © 1973, 1978, 1984 by International Bible Society. Used by permission of Hodder & Stoughton, a division of Hodder Headline Ltd. All rights reserved.

'NIV' is a registered trademark of International Bible Society. UK trademark number 1448790.

Printed and bound in Italy by Grafica Veneta S.p.A.

*And so Jesus also suffered
outside the city gate
to make the people holy through his own blood*
(Hebrews 13:12).

Contents

		Page
Acknowledgements		9
Introduction — Sin is a big deal		11
1.	Faith alone — reason for joy!	21
2.	Penal substitution — how we can be forgiven and forgive	37
3.	Justification — right with God	54
4.	Imputed righteousness — a legal fiction?	68
5.	Christ's obedience — all that God requires	85
6.	Sanctification — shall we go on sinning?	104
Epilogue — Outside the city		119
Notes		125

Acknowledgements

THIS book began as a series of messages to the congregation of Chertsey Street in Guildford over the autumn Sunday mornings of 2009.

I first of all wish to acknowledge my indebtedness to the church for all their encouragement and patience. Indeed it was through the especially warm response I received to these expositions from many in the church, particularly Rose Smith and Peter Rush, that I was motivated to write.

Secondly, I am indebted to many other books and authors as I have worked on the material I have brought together here. Notably included among them are the works of Professor John Murray, Professor Donald Macleod and the authors of the book *By Faith Alone* (Crossway) which I have leaned on heavily, especially the contribution of David VanDrunen in chapter 5.

Thirdly, I also want to thank the people who were prepared to let me use their stories in this book to illustrate the solid joys and lasting treasures of personally knowing salvation through the Lord Jesus Christ. I have included such testimonies to God's grace at the end of each chapter in order that readers might get a personal taste of the delightful reality of the gospel. What we are handling are not dry doctrines, but exhilarating, life-changing truths.

Most of all, of course, I am indebted to the Lord Jesus Christ, who shed his own blood to establish our salvation and, therefore, the great evangelical doctrines of the New

Testament which are such a thrill and source of hope to sinners and which I have endeavoured to explain and release onto the following pages.

> Worthy is the Lamb, who was slain,
> to receive power and wealth and wisdom and strength
> and honour and glory and praise!

John Benton
Guildford

Introduction
Sin is a big deal

THERE is a story which makes me smile and which says a lot about how undiscerning human beings can be. Back in the earlier part of the twentieth century, silent movies drew large audiences, and one of the megastars of the silent screen was the slapstick comedian Charlie Chaplin, famous for his baggy trousers, bowler hat and toothbrush moustache. The story is that, in the state of Illinois in the USA, there was once a Charlie Chaplin lookalike competition. But, unbeknown to anyone, Charlie Chaplin himself entered the competition just for a bit of fun. The result? It was a classic moment. He came third!

This incident acts as a parable for the contemporary church. These days there are many competitors and 'lookalikes' around for the gospel of Christ. And the tragedy is that there is such a measure of confusion and lack of discernment in the churches that we are often unable to recognize the genuine article when we see it. The good news of the New Testament comes in a creditable third with many church people. It is regarded as just one among quite a few options for the church's message. It is being replaced, even in the thinking of many Christians, by rather deceptive lookalikes of various kinds.

Heartbeat of the gospel

The central burden of this book is to go back to some key passages of Scripture and rediscover, restate and rejoice in the breathtaking reality of what the cross of Christ achieved, which is the gospel as preached by the apostles. By this I mean gospel truths such as salvation by faith alone, the cross of Christ as a penal substitution and Christ's righteousness being credited to us. Singling out certain truths and Bible passages might give the impression of jumping from one thing to another rather than making for a smooth read. But an army has to defend its position by concentrating on the points in its line where it is being attacked, not elsewhere, and at present we are seeing the gospel assailed at various key points, rather than facing an offensive over a broad front.

The very truths under attack, over which so much confusion and controversy have arisen in recent years, are those truths which I personally find the most exhilarating and God-glorifying. Who could not be excited, for example, by the fact that salvation is by faith alone, or that the Son of God died in our place to eradicate the punishment we deserved? These things are a continual wonder to me. In business terms we tend to think in Britain of 'big deals' being done 'in the city', the square mile which forms the financial district of London. But the biggest deals of all, those which secure eternal riches for sinners, moral bankrupts like us, were done 'outside the city'. They were achieved by the Lord Jesus Christ at the cross. Outside the city wall of Jerusalem was where 'the dear Lord' was crucified.

However, sadly, as already noted, these things which have formed the very heartbeat of gospel proclamation for evangelicals for many centuries have fallen under a shadow. Those of us who do cling to these classic doctrines and believe that they really are important are often looked at askance by others. We find ourselves now, like Christ and his cross, 'outside the city', disowned by the secular world and even by professing Christians who see themselves as more flexible on such matters.

I believe the setting aside of, or failure to defend, these truths is a grave mistake. Such things are actually God's big deals which alone 'do the business' for us as sinners. They are the truth which makes salvation a rock-solid certainty for all who trust Christ. When properly understood they set believing hearts on fire with love for Christ and provide a sure foundation for radical Christian discipleship. They show us 'How deep the Father's love for us' and just how far he has been prepared to go in his grace. The central reason for writing this book is simply to bring these wonderful gospel doctrines into the light again.

Changing culture

What is the reason for the attacks upon, and uncertainty over, these vital areas of the gospel? My own suspicion is that, though there may be various secondary contributory factors, the major cause is to be found in a covert revolution in Western culture which has been gradually changing people's thinking. This shift in the way we approach life has come very subtly and taken many Christian people almost unawares.

What is this change? We have moved from a moral culture to what I will call a culture of emotion. This change can be understood fairly simply. Whereas previously the word 'good' was defined in terms of 'right' and 'wrong', these days the idea of what is 'good' is much more likely to be understood in terms of what 'feels good'. Things are good if they make you happy. Let me give some examples which indicate this move.

You can see this change very simply, for example, in the way the word 'wicked' has changed its meaning at the popular level. During the 1990s it was released from its standard meaning of denoting something which is morally bad. Instead it has come to mean something which is exciting and will give you a high. One of the Bible writers speaks of 'the pleasures of sin' (Hebrews 11:25), and that 'pleasure', or 'feel-good' factor, is perceived as good. So 'wicked' now means 'good' (see Isaiah 5:20).

You can see this change also in, for example, the area of parenting. Recently I heard of a parenting course which insisted that we must never tell children that they are 'naughty', or that some of their choices are 'bad' in the old moral sense. 'There are no "good" or "bad" choices; there are only "happy" or "sad" choices,' those attending the course were told. Do you see the shift?

At the more serious level Professor Frank Furedi has described and chronicled the rise of the new way of thinking in his book *Therapy Culture*. The culture of emotion is the outcome of secularism. Secularism (which denies God's existence, or at least his relevance to everyday life) believes that there is no overall meaning or absolute truth about the world. Hence there is no faith or ideology worth living for, so living for self and feeling good about oneself become the only possible purpose for life. This is at the root of the shift from a moral culture to an emotional one. Furedi presents, among other things, statistical evidence underlining the reality of this culture shift. He tells us, for example, that a search of 300 UK newspapers in 1980 did not find a single reference to the term 'self-esteem'. It found three citations in 1986. By 1990 this figure rose to 103. A decade later, in 2000, there were a staggering 3,328 references. Similar figures apply for words like 'trauma' and 'stress'. This is the language of emotion and of therapy for damaged emotions. The old way of keeping a 'stiff upper lip' and not letting your feelings show is decried. We are encouraged to wear our hearts on our sleeves, let our feelings show and be 'authentic'.

Introduction

Feeling good

Again, this culture shift is seen in the way people have become much more 'touchy/feely' than before. We are the children of the *Friends* TV series generation. The emphasis upon feeling good has put a premium on choosing and making personal relationships with others because it is those relationships which are often the avenues along which the 'feel-good' factor comes to us. To be with our group of *amigos* is where we feel accepted and loved. This makes us happy. These days when friends meet the mere handshake of recognition is often not enough. There are far more hugs between male buddies. There are cheek-to-cheek kisses among the women. These gestures are meant to signify how intensely we love and are loved. There is nothing wrong with this at all so long as it is genuine. But it simply highlights how personal relationships, and the emotions we experience and express in and through those relationships, have become much more important to people.

In the new culture, life is not about making right moral choices. It is about relationships and feelings. We interpret normal experience through the medium of an emotional rather than a moral script. 'How did that make you feel?' asks the TV interviewer. We now take emotions very seriously and morals not so seriously, because they are seen as not absolute but just matters of opinion.

Now, Christians being people for whom love is of primary concern (1 Corinthians 13:1-3), it is very easy for us to buy into this culture of emotion. We like to make people feel better, and at one level, of course, that is extremely commendable. But often we have not thought this thing through. We have not understood where the culture of emotion which so influences us is actually coming from. Think about this illustration. Suppose a drug which a doctor prescribes makes the patient feel better but actually makes his underlying condition much worse. What then?

THE PROBLEM OF SIN

To get to the heart of the matter, the biblical gospel is predicated upon the truth that mankind's deepest problem is a moral one — the problem of sin. The most fundamental truth about God is that he is holy. Before God's throne it is not first of all his love, but his holiness, that the angels declare in their worship (Isaiah 6:3; Revelation 4:8). And that holiness has a stridently moral aspect which condemns sin and sinners (Isaiah 6:5).

We are those who have broken God's moral law. We are those who are rebels against that which is right, as defined by God's holy character, and biased towards that which is wrong. Scripture frames the human condition in terms of the consequences of Adam's disobedience towards our Maker and our God. Yes, our moral rebellion has brought many bad emotional consequences, such as feeling insecure. But because mankind's central problem is one of moral failure, salvation must take place first and foremost in moral terms, not emotional. Law is broken. Justice must be satisfied. Reparation must be made. Forgiveness and righteousness are required. And so it goes on. This is all very uncomfortable — not to say alien — in our current culture, where morality and law are caricatured as being 'cold' and 'judgemental' in their very essence.

My thesis is that the major cause of our current confusion about the gospel is that the culture of emotion has influenced the thinking of Christians far more than we realize. Because we now tend to read Scripture through emotional rather than moral spectacles, we have come to feel uncomfortable about truths like penal substitution and the imputation of Christ's righteousness to the sinner. We would like to think either that what were previously regarded as some of the central tenets of evangelical faith have been misunderstood, or else that we can dispense with them without doing much harm.

But the thrust of Scripture is that sin is a big deal. The primary problem for the human race is a moral one. It is sin which has ruined the world and brought suffering and death and the prospect of a lost eternity. 'The wrath of God is being revealed from heaven against all the godlessness and wickedness of men' (Romans 1:18).

New Perspective

There are, of course, other strands feeding into all of this. Some would tell us that the changes being contemplated for the gospel have come about because of academic advances in understanding the Bible. We are told, for example, that the Reformers, on whose work so much of evangelical thinking has been based, had not properly understood the Jewish background of the first century against which St Paul, for example, wrote his epistles and therefore they misinterpreted the apostle.

But there are two things to say about this.

First, I am sure that there have been academic advances over recent years. For example, the work of E. P. Sanders on first-century Jewish faith (Second Temple Judaism, as it is called) has been a major contribution. He understands first-century Judaism in terms of 'covenantal nomism'. It means that God was gracious to Israel in selecting them as his people, conferring on them the privilege of a relationship with him and giving them his covenant. But it was by Israel's keeping of God's law that they were to keep themselves in the covenant. This understanding is helpful but, as far as I can see, doesn't actually change much. Here we have a classic religion which mixes both God's grace and people's good works. Theologically it is a breed of semi-Pelagianism, which is precisely what the Reformers fought against. For comment on this mixture of grace and works, see later in this book. However, it is out of this seedbed that the so-called New Perspective on Paul has grown. This movement (which I will refer to as the NPP for brevity) is difficult to characterize completely, but it is generally agreed that it includes the following ideas:

- The gospel is that 'Jesus is Lord', not first of all that he is the Saviour of sinners.
- The 'righteousness of God' is a technical term denoting God's covenant faithfulness.
- Justification is about how people are included within the covenant people of God, rather than to do with being right (in a moral sense) with God.
- The word 'righteous' is understood as a kind of code word describing those who are included in the covenant. They are 'the righteous'.
- Paul's disagreement with the Jews, expressed in his epistles, was not about how people get right with God; it was more to do with the Jewish resistance to including the Gentiles in God's covenant.

My concern is not so much about the new research into first-century Judaism as that, from a perusal of the main thrusts of the NPP, its direction looks suspiciously similar to that of the current culture of emotion which so subtly influences us. Look at that list. The gospel is not first of all about Christ's dealing with sin. So the gospel is not primarily about a moral problem. The 'righteousness of God', which naturally invokes a moral understanding, is restricted to relational/covenantal terms. Again, the ideas of justification and righteousness are reinterpreted in relational rather than moral terms. Though I am in no position to dispute the data which modern academic research has thrown up concerning first-century Judaism, there is more than a suggestion that such data has been interpreted, albeit unconsciously, in a way which is rather too conveniently in tune with the world's prevailing culture of emotion.

INTRODUCTION 19

I am suggesting that the influence of the prevailing culture puts pressures even on Christian academics to reshape the gospel in ways which distort the apostolic message.

A FIRST-CENTURY EYEWITNESS

Secondly, one of the main accusations of the NPP against the evangelical theology of the Reformers is that they had not understood, as our generation has understood, that first-century Judaism was actually a religion of grace, not of works. The Reformers are accused of reading the problems they had with the medieval Roman Catholic Church back into the New Testament.

However, for me one of the indications that NPP enthusiasts may not have read the data correctly is not only the way the Lord Jesus portrays the Pharisees as legalistic in the Gospels (e.g., Matthew 23:4-32), but the way that the first-century Jewish historian Josephus portrays Jewish religion. Here are a few quotes from him about the Pharisees:

> The Pharisees count as the leading Jewish sect. Their opinion is that what God wills is what happens, yet men are free to act as they think fit, virtuously or viciously. They believe in the immortality of the soul and in rewards and punishments after death. They say that those who live virtuously will have power to live again, but those who have lived viciously will be detained in an everlasting prison. The mass of the population, persuaded of the truth of these doctrines, perform whatever the Pharisees prescribe and divine worship, prayers and sacrifices. On account of their teaching and their good conduct the Pharisees are greatly respected. Unlike the Sadducees, they are friendly to each other and seek to promote concord with the general public.

They delivered to the people a great many observances which are not written in the law of Moses at all but derived from their ancestors. They were specially believed when they spoke severely against others, even though it was only due to envy.[1]

I am not supposing that Josephus was a totally unbiased observer. However, it seems much more likely that he, as an eyewitness of first-century Jewish religion, would have a clearer view of it than we have from the distance of two thousand years or so. Josephus is explicit that the religion of the Pharisees boiled down, at least at a popular level, to a religion of works. No doubt there was some idea of grace mixed in there too. But when it comes to salvation, Josephus says that it was a matter of reward for virtuous living. This again indicates that the Reformers were not so off-beam after all in their approach to the New Testament and to what the dispute over the gospel between Paul and the Jews was really about.

Enough by way of introduction. Let's proceed to look at some of the vital truths concerning the apostolic gospel. While we will from time to time address some of the issues raised by the NPP, our main aim will be to be encouraged by the sheer grace of God in Christ.

Big deal 1
Faith alone — reason for joy!

ROMANS 3:21-31

But now a righteousness from God, apart from law, has been made known, to which the Law and the Prophets testify. This righteousness from God comes through faith in Jesus Christ to all who believe. There is no difference, for all have sinned and fall short of the glory of God, and are justified freely by his grace through the redemption that came by Christ Jesus. God presented him as a sacrifice of atonement, through faith in his blood. He did this to demonstrate his justice, because in his forbearance he had left the sins committed beforehand unpunished — he did it to demonstrate his justice at the present time, so as to be just and the one who justifies those who have faith in Jesus.

Where, then, is boasting? It is excluded. On what principle? On that of observing the law? No, but on that of faith. For we maintain that a man is justified by faith apart from observing the law. Is God the God of Jews only? Is he not the God of Gentiles too? Yes, of Gentiles too, since there is only one God, who will justify the circumcised by faith and the uncircumcised through that same faith. Do we, then, nullify the law by this faith? Not at all! Rather, we uphold the law.

RICHARD was a much-loved trainee pastor with our congregation. As I write he and his wife Telda lead a church of their own. If you ever hear Richard tell the story of how he became a Christian he will tell you that the first time he heard and properly understood the gospel, he literally danced around the room.

This is not the kind of thing that well-bred Englishmen usually do. We tend to be too reserved for that sort of thing. But Richard danced.

It was such wonderful news to him that he couldn't contain himself. What he had understood was that Jesus Christ, through his life, death and resurrection, has done everything, absolutely everything, required for our forgiveness and acceptance with God, and now God accepts us by faith alone. All we have to do is trust Jesus. We don't need to merit anything. We don't need to worry or fret about how 'holy' we might feel or whether we have been to church enough. We don't need to total up how many hours we have spent in prayer, or how many good deeds we have done each day, to try to earn God's favour. Faith alone (and I'm talking about faith in Jesus Christ) does the trick.

Faith is an open hand, and when we open that hand towards Jesus, into it God places this astonishing free gift of forgiveness and eternal salvation.

Churchianity and Christianity

Richard had been brought up in church religion which has come adrift from the real good news of Jesus. This basically says that the good go to heaven and the bad go to hell, and so to find acceptance with God you had better be good. Some Christians call this 'Churchianity' because it is not the real Christianity of the New Testament. It has more to do with formal church — like collection plates, confirmation, confessionals and conformity — than with Christ.

Churchianity says, 'Yes, Jesus has done his bit, but now you had better do yours, or else.' But Richard knew he wasn't always good, and anyway no one could tell him how good he had to be. What was the passmark which would merit entrance to heaven? Richard could never find out. So he could never be sure that he had done enough. And even if he felt he had done quite well one day, what about the next? It was a continual worry. So religion had become a crushing burden to him. It was a life of unhappy uncertainty with the threat of damnation forever hanging over his head if he missed the mark in any way. It was legalistic, joyless drudgery.

But at that meeting where he heard the good news, he was shown from the New Testament that this religion of trying to keep the rules, and so merit God's favour, is not the gospel. He saw that we are saved by faith alone. A hymn, beloved by many Christians, puts the good news of the gospel like this:

> The vilest offender who truly believes
> that moment from Jesus a pardon receives.

It is this glorious message of salvation through faith alone which Paul is announcing and defending in this passage at the end of Romans 3.

GOD'S COMMANDS

Earlier in his letter to the church in Rome Paul has explained that, left to ourselves, the reason we are not acceptable to God is our sin — all the wrong things we have done, in thought, word and deed, which, worryingly, somehow come so naturally to us all. Our sin means that we don't keep the rules and that we lack righteousness before a holy God. Righteousness is a life which measures up to God's law, in particular the Ten Commandments. In case you have forgotten them, the Ten Commandments tell us:

- We are to have no other God but the God of the Bible.
- We are not to worship idols (whether the primitive sort or the sophisticated Western kind).
- We are not to misuse God's name.

- We are to keep God's day holy.
- We are to honour our parents.
- We are not to murder (in deed or thought).
- We are not to commit adultery (neither the act nor in our imagination).
- We are not to steal.
- We are not to tell lies.
- We are not to covet things that don't belong to us.

There are many other laws in the Old Testament, but these are special. This is shown by the fact that these ten 'words' were spoken by the very voice of God from Mount Sinai to Moses, and that they were written on the tablets of stone by 'the finger of God' and kept in the ark of the covenant. The other commands were not. The Ten Commandments are of abiding importance to us all. It is these ten commands that Paul clearly has in mind when he tells us later in Romans that Christian love fulfils the law (Romans 13:8-10).

Moral failure

But all of us, Jews and Gentiles, are sinners, rebels against that law. If we measure ourselves up against these commands we find that we fail — totally. Who is the person who has never told a lie? Where is the man who has never had an adulterous thought? Where is the woman who has never been envious of what another person has? Who has always treated God with the honour he deserves? There are no such people. We are all morally flawed. All the law can do is condemn us:

> Now we know that whatever the law says, it says to those who are under the law, so that every mouth may be silenced and the whole world held accountable to

God. Therefore no one will be declared righteous in his sight by observing the law; rather, through the law we become conscious of sin (Romans 3:19-20).

Notice that, even though it was given by God explicitly to the Jews, Paul assumes here that the law is for *the whole world* — all mankind. (The law's requirements are actually written on the hearts of each one of us — see Romans 2:15). Even the very best of our deeds — our charitable gifts, our selfless acts — are in themselves like 'filthy rags' (Isaiah 64:6) in God's sight because they are energized by motives other than pleasing God. This leaves us in dire trouble. We know we ought to keep the law, but we find that we can never match up to it. If we are honest, we realize we are moral failures. So, as Richard found, a religion of merit, of legalism, can only leave us feeling crushed.

But Christ came

Is there any hope for us? Astonishingly the answer is 'Yes!' according to the apostle Paul. But it is not through the law; it is through Christ and his gospel. This is where we begin to look at the text quoted at the beginning of this chapter. Through Jesus Christ the most unexpected thing has happened. There is a righteousness which is the gift of God, promised in the Old Testament and now become a reality through Jesus and his cross. We naturally think that righteousness is about how we behave. We imagine it is based on what we have done. If righteousness came by the law, that would be true. But in Christ, God has done something completely new. This is what Paul says:

> But now a righteousness from God, apart from law, has been made known, to which the Law and the Prophets testify. This righteousness from God comes

through faith in Jesus Christ to all who believe (Romans 3:21-22).

There is now a righteousness which is not 'from us' (by our deeds) but which comes 'from God' and is given as a gift.

At the cross Christ, by his death, answers two great problems we have.

First, *we have broken God's law*. But at the cross Jesus paid the penalty we deserved for our lawbreaking, so atoning for our sins (v. 23). He did this for everyone and anyone who believes.

Secondly, *we have not obeyed God*; we have therefore not lived the kind of life that would bring God the honour that is rightfully his. But at the cross Jesus obeyed and honoured God to the uttermost on behalf of all who believe, so that God can declare us righteous in his sight — in other words, justify us (v. 26).

We will say more about this in the following chapters. But for the moment the point to grasp is that it is all about faith. God's gift of righteousness is given to those who believe. Four times in verses 21-26 belief or faith in Jesus is mentioned as the key.

Faith?

Before we go any further there is something we need to clear up. What is faith? This is a key question. The New Testament tells us that it is personal trust in Christ. Perhaps it is best exemplified through the miracles of Jesus. Take the case of that woman with the issue of blood whom the doctors could not cure, and this had gone on for twelve years. She drew near to Jesus, saying to herself, 'If I just touch his clothes, I will be healed' (Mark 5:28). She knew she had no ability whatsoever to cure herself. All her trust was in Jesus. On the basis of the evidence of the reports of his previous miracles, she believed in him and his power. And it was in that context that after she was healed Jesus said to her, 'Daughter, your faith has healed you' (Mark 5:34). For us, similarly, it is faith, personal trust in Jesus Christ, that heals our relationship with God, cancelling our sin and making us acceptable to him. It is all about faith — faith alone.

Now in the verses that follow, verses 27-31, Paul makes three points which clarify this even further: first, that boasting is excluded (vv. 27-28); secondly, the inclusion of the Gentiles (vv. 29-30); and, thirdly, that the law is upheld, or established (v. 31).

BOASTING IS EXCLUDED

Since our righteous status before God is based on faith, and not on our good works at all, boasting is ruled out entirely. Look at what the apostle Paul says in our text:

> Where, then, is boasting? It is excluded. On what principle? On that of observing the law? No, but on that of faith. For we maintain that a man is justified by faith apart from observing the law (Romans 3:27-28).

We have already seen that the problem with legalistic religion based on merit and good deeds is that it crushes many sincere people because they know they always fail. But there is another side to the same coin. The other attitude that works-based religion fosters is boasting. This is because if somehow you do think you have done your bit, kept the rules enough to please God and done enough to be saved, that would make you better than others. You think you have reason to blow your own trumpet. And human nature cannot resist doing just that.

That 'holier-than-thou' assessment was the dreadful attitude of the Pharisee in the temple in Jesus' parable. As he looked around at others, he felt he was superior: 'The Pharisee stood up and prayed about himself: "God, I thank you that I am not like other men — robbers, evildoers, adulterers — or even like this tax collector. I fast twice a week and give a tenth of all I get"' (Luke 18:11-12).

Can you see what works-based religion does? A religion of merit inflates the proud and crushes the humble. Such a religion actually makes us worse people, not better. Such a religion can only damage people rather than help them. What a monstrosity! How could this ever honour God? This is not the gospel. It is so important to understand this point that I will say it again: this is *not* the gospel.

But we need to understand something more. Notice that this is the case if there is *any* degree of good deeds or merit necessary for our salvation. Even if Christ paid 95% of our salvation, but left us to produce the last 5%, there would still be cause for some to trumpet their achievements and for others to feel that they had failed. Even if he left us with only 1% to perform ourselves, it would be the same. Still some would feel superior for having completed their percentage and others would worry that they still could not match up. This is how human nature is. No. What Paul says in these verses means that our good deeds, our law-keeping, have no place whatsoever in meriting our salvation. Boasting is excluded because merit is excluded. Salvation is by faith alone. It is by faith alone because Christ has done it all.

'Faith alone, *sola fide*' was one of the great slogans of the Reformation as Europe rediscovered the joy and wonder of the biblical gospel during the sixteenth century. Salvation really is by faith alone. This is wonderful news. This is what caused my friend Richard to dance for joy.

THE GENTILES ARE INCLUDED

Paul now brings a second argument to underline that justification, being counted right with God, is by faith alone. His argument in our text is that the oneness of God demands that Jews and Gentiles must be justified in the same way — that is, by faith:

> Is God the God of Jews only? Is he not the God of Gentiles too? Yes, of Gentiles too, since there is only one God, who will justify the circumcised by faith and the uncircumcised through that same faith (Romans 3:29-30).

Paul here employs the best-known verse in Judaism, the *Shema* (Deuteronomy 6:4). It says this: 'Hear, O Israel: The LORD our God, the LORD is one.' It is the classic statement of monotheism, and Paul argues from that great premise.

If there is only one God, then surely he is the God of the whole world, not only of the Jews. The Old Testament looked forward to the day when the Gentiles would come to worship the true God. Israel was to be a light for the Gentiles to lead them to the Lord, and this would be fulfilled, says Isaiah, in the true Israel, the Suffering Servant (Isaiah 42:6). The Psalms are full of encouragements to declare God's glory among the nations, and speak of all peoples rejoicing in the Lord (see, e.g., Psalm 67).

Such Old Testament verses must have puzzled many Jews: 'How can the Gentiles be acceptable to God? They don't have the law. They have not been given the Old Testament as we have. The only way they can come to God is if they cease to be Gentiles and become Jews like us, taking on our way of life.' Indeed, that would be true if righteousness came by the law. But Paul is declaring a new kind of righteousness. He is telling us that in Christ righteousness comes not by the law, but as the gift of God into the hands of faith. And faith has no necessity for the law.

'Well,' says Paul to his Jewish kinsmen, 'what's the answer to your conundrum? Can't you see that the universalism of God's lordship over all peoples requires a gospel about a righteousness that comes apart from law? Can't you see that it demands a gospel about a righteousness that comes by faith?'

Look at it another way. Paul has already explained in verses 19-20 that the Jews could not actually keep the law themselves, so how could they expect the Gentiles to find righteousness through law? No. The old covenant is over; the new covenant has come, with its offer of salvation to all the world.

Faith in Christ, rather than the Jewish mark of circumcision (v. 30), is decisive for inclusion among the people of God, because it is by faith in Christ that we are counted righteous in God's sight. That there is one God implies one way of salvation. And that can only be by faith in Christ. (By the way, that change of preposition in verse 30, 'by faith' for the Jews and 'through faith' for the uncircumcised Gentiles, is purely stylistic and is of no theological import, as the fact that Paul emphasizes that it is the *same* faith makes clear.)

It is faith — faith alone, without any good works or Jewish trappings. This, of course, is what Paul had to fight and argue through in his epistle to the Galatians, where, essentially, false teachers were saying that it was acceptable for Gentiles to become Christians as long as they became Jews first. 'No,' says Paul, 'if you put your trust in being circumcised it implies an obligation to keep the whole law, and so you are back where you started. Christ is then of no use to you. It is all of faith — faith alone' (see Galatians 5:2).

THE LAW IS UPHELD

Now, having positively argued for faith alone, lastly Paul rebuts an objection which, it seems, had been frequently directed at him and his teaching. The objection goes like this: 'With all this emphasis on faith alone, does that mean, Paul, that you are doing away completely with God's law and that Christians can live as they please?' Look at what our text says in verse 31: 'Do we ... nullify the law by this faith? Not at all! Rather, we uphold the law.'

How is the law established, or upheld, through faith? There are two things to say.

First, the law is established because *Christ obeyed it all in full on our behalf.* 'In no way am I saying,' says Paul, 'that the law is of no consequence.' How did Jesus live his life? He fully and perfectly kept the law. Why did Jesus die? It was to pay the penalty that the law demands. God's law stands.

Secondly, though our salvation is through Christ by faith alone, *the moral norms of the law still function as the authoritative will of God for the believer.* Right is still right. We don't obey the law in order to be saved. But because we are saved we want to keep the law out of thankfulness to God, and the Holy Spirit helps us in this. This is what Paul spells out later on in Romans. For example, look at Romans 8:1-4:

> Therefore, there is now no condemnation for those who are in Christ Jesus... For what the law was powerless to do in that it was weakened by the sinful nature, God did by sending his own Son in the likeness of sinful man to be a sin offering. And so he condemned sin in sinful man, in order that the righteous requirements of the law might be fully met in us, who do not live according to the sinful nature but according to the Spirit.

Here we see that part of the purpose of our being saved (note, the *result* of salvation, not the *cause* of salvation) is that we might keep the law.

This comes about as we increasingly live the life of Christian love which will be perfected in God's kingdom. Look again at Romans 13:8-10: 'Let no debt remain outstanding, except the continuing debt to love one another, for he who loves his fellow-man has fulfilled the law...'

So in no way is Paul saying that the law is nullified. Rather, he shows that it plays no part in meriting our salvation — which is by faith alone.

Faith and works?

Now this enables us to see clearly a couple of things which are very important.

First, we see *the difference between the true gospel and false religion*. It is the difference between real Christianity and the 'Churchianity' we mentioned at the outset of the chapter. This difference can be expressed quite clearly by two equations which I have always found very helpful. False religion can be summarized in the equation: faith + works = salvation. Paul says that is false religion: 'For we maintain that a man is justified by faith apart from observing the law' (v. 28). But the true faith, real Christianity, the apostolic gospel, is seen in the equation: faith = salvation + good works. Faith in Christ gives us eternal life, salvation. But that eternal life begins to show itself in the here and now as our lives are changed. Those changed lives include our being involved in good works out of love for Christ who has saved us. We are not saved *by* our good works, but we are saved *for* good works, as we saw in Romans 8:4 (see also Ephesians 2:8-10).

Secondly, those good works in no way contribute to meriting our salvation, but the Christian does good works out of thankfulness to God that we have been saved and they become *an evidence of salvation and of the genuineness of our faith*. If we really believe, God's Spirit will come into our hearts and our lives will change. Understanding this harmonizes what at first sight seems to be a conflict between Paul and James.

Paul and James?

Paul says, 'For we maintain that a man is justified by faith apart from observing the law' (Romans 3:28). But when we read the New Testament letter of James we find that James says, 'You see that a person is justified by what he does and not by faith alone' (James 2:24).

What is going on here? They seem to be saying the opposite of one another. But the answer is actually very simple. The word 'justify' (as we shall see in more depth in a later chapter) means to be declared in line with the law of the court. If you look at the context of what Paul is saying and what James is saying, you will find that the 'courts' in which they are operating are somewhat different.

Paul is talking about the fundamental question of how people are put right with the holy God. This is the court of morality, the court of right and wrong in the sight of God. In that great court people are counted right purely through faith in Christ and what he has done. It is through faith alone — Jesus has done it all.

But that is not James' prime concern. His concern is the related but different question: 'How do you know faith is genuine?' James is operating not in the court of morality (right and wrong), but in the court of authenticity (true or false). Paul is at the law courts; James is at Sotheby's the auctioneers. This is where works of art are up for sale, and people are asking, 'Is this the real thing, or is it a fake?', 'Is this an authentic Rembrandt or not?' James' question is: 'Is this person's faith genuine or not?' His point is that true faith will show itself in good deeds. Paul would say 'Amen' to that. 'Can we go on living in sin once we are saved? By no means!' (see Romans 6:2). We are saved so that 'the righteous requirements of the law might be fully met in us' (Romans 8:4). But we are saved by faith alone.

Authentic Christianity

It is this same understanding that gives the key to Christ's great parable of the sheep and the goats which we find in Matthew's Gospel and which looks forward to Judgement Day.

In Matthew 25:31-46 Jesus tells of all people being assembled before him and being divided as a shepherd divides the sheep from the goats. The sheep are saved; the goats are lost. The basis for the division is how different people have treated the 'brothers' of Christ.

On the surface the parable of the sheep and the goats appears to tell us of a judgement based on works. Who visited the prisoners, or gave hospitality to the stranger, and who didn't?

But, if we look at it closely, we find that it isn't quite like that. Jesus says, 'The King will reply, "I tell you the truth, whatever you did for one of the least of these brothers of mine, you did for me"' (Matthew 25:40). Christ's brothers are of course, Christian people (Mark 3:34). In other words, it is not the works that merit their salvation but, rather, these works of kindness to Christ's people are the things that show their connection to Christ. They do good to Christ's people, quite unconsciously, because they trust and love Christ. The genuineness of their faith in Christ is shown by the way they have treated other believers. It is Jesus who does the saving, and these works show that they belong to Jesus.

To illustrate the point, think of a car park where you must 'pay and display'. You pay for a ticket and then you display the fact that your car-parking space has been paid for by sticking the ticket on the windscreen. But think about it. The money pays the tariff for the parking space; the ticket confirms that the tariff has been paid. The ticket itself pays for nothing. Rather, it simply shows that the car has been paid for. In the same way, Christ alone paid for our sins and

Faith alone

put us right with God, and our changed lives (of faith and consequent good deeds) simply show that we are the ones he has saved. He did the paying. Our good works don't pay for anything. They simply show that we are Christ's.

It is not faith + good deeds = salvation. It is faith = salvation + good deeds. We are saved by faith alone. Nothing else is required. The gospel really is the best news in the world. It is God's music to set our hearts dancing.

What's the big deal for me?

The joyful big deal for us as individuals which this chapter has tried to spell out is that salvation is a free gift. It is not given according to our deserving, but is put into the hands of all who simply believe.

To illustrate what this can mean for a person, let me tell you the story of how Telda, the wife of Richard, whom we have already met in this chapter, came to Christ.

Telda's brother was already a Christian. When she followed him to Britain from South Africa she sought him out and he invited her to attend a six-week course about Christianity. 'I went along, but only to please my brother,' Telda says.

Week one, there was no problem. They discussed the historical reliability of the Bible.

Week two was similarly straightforward. It was about how great God is. She thought, 'I figured that if there is a God out there he must be outrageously clever to make this universe.'

Week three, however, they hit a major problem! They were shown that 'All have sinned and fall short of the glory of God.' Telda was furious: 'How dare someone call me a sinner? I try my best. I might have misbehaved a few times, but I've never murdered anyone! There are far more unpleasant people out there than me!'

Week four, things only got worse. It was explained that the Bible tells us that 'Man is destined to die once, and after that to face judgement.' She did not like the idea of judgement one little bit. Where was this great God of love Christians always went on about? She found the whole message unpalatable and threatening. She decided that this was the end of the course for her. She would not go again.

But somehow, very reluctantly, she returned for week five. What happened? This is what she says: 'What I expected to get next was a set of rules about me pulling my socks up and being a better person. But what I heard was exactly the opposite. I heard that because God loved me so much, he was prepared to do something astonishing about my predicament. His plan was hugely costly to him. God's Son, Jesus, was punished for all the wrong things that I had ever thought, said and done. That was why Jesus came to earth: to willingly die — for me! I couldn't believe what I was hearing! Here was indeed a God of love.' It was the freeness of God's salvation which took her breath away.

'It was hard decision time. And yet one thing was crystal clear,' she recalls. 'If the Maker and Ruler of the universe really died for me, how could I go on living without acknowledging him? By the time the last week arrived I didn't need more convincing. There was a lot I didn't know, but there was enough I was sure about to know that I wanted "in". Within days I knew that Jesus was the love of my life. I saw the world through new eyes. The lifestyle change was enormous, and yet I gained a new friend — the King of the universe!'

You cannot miss the joy and grateful wonder in all that Telda says here. Praise God for such a salvation!

Big deal 2
Penal substitution — how we can be forgiven and forgive

ISAIAH 53

Who has believed our message
    and to whom has the arm of the Lord been revealed?
He grew up before him like a tender shoot,
    and like a root out of dry ground.
He had no beauty or majesty to attract us to him,
    nothing in his appearance that we should desire him.
He was despised and rejected by men,
    a man of sorrows, and familiar with suffering.
Like one from whom men hide their faces
    he was despised, and we esteemed him not.
Surely he took up our infirmities
    and carried our sorrows,
yet we considered him stricken by God,
    smitten by him, and afflicted.
But he was pierced for our transgressions,
    he was crushed for our iniquities;
the punishment that brought us peace was upon him,
    and by his wounds we are healed.
We all, like sheep, have gone astray,
    each of us has turned to his own way;
and the Lord has laid on him
    the iniquity of us all.
He was oppressed and afflicted,
    yet he did not open his mouth;

> he was led like a lamb to the slaughter,
> > and as a sheep before her shearers is silent,
> > so he did not open his mouth.
> By oppression and judgement he was taken away.
> > And who can speak of his descendants?
> For he was cut off from the land of the living;
> > for the transgression of my people he was stricken.
> He was assigned a grave with the wicked,
> > and with the rich in his death,
> though he had done no violence,
> > nor was any deceit in his mouth.
> Yet it was the LORD's will to crush him and cause him to suffer,
> > and though the LORD makes his life a guilt offering,
> he will see his offspring and prolong his days,
> > and the will of the LORD will prosper in his hand.
> After the suffering of his soul,
> > he will see the light [of life] and be satisfied;
> by his knowledge my righteous servant will justify many,
> > and he will bear their iniquities.
> Therefore I will give him a portion among the great,
> > and he will divide the spoils with the strong,
> because he poured out his life unto death,
> > and was numbered with the transgressors.
> For he bore the sin of many,
> > and made intercession for the transgressors.

The Rev. Julie Nicholson sadly lost her daughter Jenny at the Edgware Road tube station in the suicide bomber attacks of July 2005 in London. In March the following year she resigned from her clergy post because she found it too hard to forgive the terrorist murderers. 'It is a very difficult time for me,' she said, 'to celebrate the Eucharist and lead people in words of peace and reconciliation and forgiveness when I feel very far from that myself.' One feels the greatest sympathy for her along with a real admiration for her transparent integrity displayed in her decision to resign. She felt she couldn't go on calling on people to forgive others when she herself couldn't forgive.

I don't want to comment on her particular case, but it made me wonder at the time whether the general undermining of the New Testament gospel, and in particular of Christ's death as a penal substitution — that is, Christ bearing in our place the punishment that we sinners deserve — makes it much harder for us to forgive others and act as Christians.

A SENSE OF RIGHT AND WRONG

Where am I coming from? All people, made in the image of God, have a deep moral sense of right and wrong. From our earliest years we find ourselves saying, 'That's not fair,' when we sense that things are not right. And though we now live in a culture of emotion which plays down and suppresses moral concerns, nevertheless when people suffer unspeakable injustice — as in the killing of an innocent traveller, like Julie Nicholson's daughter — those connected with the victims suffer more than just hurt. The priority of morality is forced back to the surface. The enormity of the tragedy causes them to look beyond their feelings to the injustice of what has happened. They experience a legitimate and powerful moral indignation, a righteous fury, which goes to the very roots of their being. They cry, 'This is not fair. This is not right.'

So, for example, to tell the parents of the schoolchildren killed at Beslan in September 2004, or the relatives of other innocent people killed by terrorists, that God is all 'love' and that no one will pay for the atrocity, but they must simply forgive, is to ask them to contravene the deepest foundations of what they are as people. A gospel of all forgiveness which finds no place for the judicial punishment of sin is actually a moral outrage. If we are preaching that, then we are saying that justice doesn't matter. No wonder that, as the liberal church has adopted this teaching, it has increasingly lost credibility with the general public.

A QUESTION OF JUSTICE

The New Testament does call us to forgive, but it does so in the context of justice done, not justice ignored. So, for example, to Christians suffering the fearful injustices of persecution Paul writes, 'Do not repay anyone evil for evil... Do not take revenge, my friends' *(*Romans 12:17,19). But why is that? What is Paul's basis for saying that? Take note of his logic in the rest of what he says: 'Do not take revenge, my friends, but leave room for God's wrath, for it is written: "It is mine to avenge; I will repay," says the Lord' (Romans 12:19). Justice is never set aside. God the Judge has a coming day of judgement. Be assured, justice will be done. No cruel dictator, no suicide bomber, no sinner at all ultimately gets away with what he or she has done. And if God will judge, that gives us a platform on which to forgive and let it drop, because right will be done in the end.

In fact Scripture assures us that when anyone does, as it were, totally 'get away with it' and is forgiven by God himself, even then justice is not ignored. They are forgiven by God only because justice has been done for their sins through Christ bearing the punishment they deserved through his death on the cross. Calvary's cross answers the question of justice.

I hope these considerations will help you to see that the matter of Christ's death as a 'penal substitution' is not some minor theological quibble. It is actually a very big deal. It goes to the centre of who God is — is he really just, or does he simply ignore injustice? It goes to the heart of our salvation — is God's forgiveness fair? And it goes to the nitty-gritty of real Christian living — are we able to find a basis for and a way of forgiving others?

Understanding what an important subject this is, in this chapter we look at Isaiah 53:4-6 to see that Scripture does teach about Christ's cross in terms of a penal substitution. There are three considerations: first, Christ's death was a substitutionary work (v. 4); secondly, Christ's death was a penal work (v. 5); and, thirdly, Christ's death was a divine work (v. 6).

Christ's death was a substitutionary work

Isaiah was writing this prophecy in the land of Judah some 700 years BC — we will pick up on the dating later. But our first question must be, 'How do we know Isaiah was talking about Jesus in what he says in the fifty-third chapter of his prophecy?'

The answer is found in Acts 8. There Philip the evangelist has been led by the Spirit to talk to an Ethiopian official who is reading from Isaiah 53. Here we have a lovely incident from the life of the early church. The evangelist Philip had been led by the Holy Spirit into meeting an official from Ethiopia (he was a eunuch) who was riding along in a chariot on his way home from Jerusalem. Philip found him reading from a scroll containing Isaiah 53, and the eunuch invited Philip to come and sit with him in the chariot and talk about what it meant. We then read, 'The eunuch asked Philip, "Tell me, please, who is the prophet talking about, himself or someone else?" Then Philip began with that very passage of Scripture and told him the good news about Jesus' (Acts 8:34-35). So the New Testament church understood Isaiah 53 as speaking of Jesus. If we are going to grasp what Isaiah had to say we must adopt this same apostolic understanding. Jesus is the Suffering Servant who so obviously fulfilled Isaiah's prophecies. So let's look at the text.

In his weighty commentary on Isaiah,[1] Alec Motyer highlights the contrast in Isaiah 53 between 'he' (God's Servant) and 'we' (God's people). In verse 4 in particular, there is 'he' and 'we', and they are not to be confused, but stand over against one another:

> Surely he took up our infirmities
>   and carried our sorrows,
> yet we considered him stricken by God,
>   smitten by him, and afflicted.

They are so separate that 'we' completely misunderstood Christ. 'We' thought 'he' was getting what 'he' deserved; in fact 'he' was doing 'us' the greatest service.

But the point to note here is how he, who is separate from us, stands in for us: 'Surely he took up our infirmities and carried our sorrows.'

The words 'took up' picture us having to carry a crushing load, but he (the Suffering Servant, Jesus) comes alongside and lifts the burden from us, takes it up himself and then carries it in our place. He did not simply stand alongside us; he got under the load instead of us. That is the picture. He substitutes himself for the burdened soul. And that substitution is highlighted by the way the word 'our' is to the fore. In the original language of the Old Testament the sentence construction is of the form, '*Our* infirmities he took up; *our* sorrows he carried.'

The Servant (Jesus) shows a great compassion in doing this. What is the burden? It is our sufferings and our sorrows. The word 'infirmities' here in verse 4 is actually the same word as 'suffering' in verse 3. Our lives are blighted with sufferings of many kinds — disappointment, tragedy, illness, guilt, and much more. But tenderly Jesus takes that load upon himself.

Moreover he takes not just our sorrows, but the cause and root of all our sufferings and sorrows — that is, human sin. We find that verse 5 goes on to speak in the same breath of our 'transgressions' and our 'iniquities' — our breaking of God's law, our corrupted human nature. The Bible tells us that God originally made all things good (Genesis 1:31). This world knew no suffering, no sorrow, until the advent of sin, which set us at odds with God our Creator. In Isaiah 53 we find that Jesus takes the whole complex of sin and its results upon himself. Verse 6 uses a similar idea to confirm our understanding of Christ taking our sins and progresses the same line of thought. It tells us not only that Jesus willingly took this complete package of sin and sorrow, but that God put these things upon him: 'The LORD has laid on him the iniquity of us all.' Our iniquities were on his shoulders. This is the language of substitution.

The reason he is able to take our sins is that he had no sin of his own:

> He was assigned a grave with the wicked,
>   and with the rich in his death,
> though he had done no violence,
>   nor was any deceit in his mouth
>
> (v. 9).

He was an innocent man, oppressed by others.

This substitutionary work of carrying our sins is spotlighted repeatedly by the apostles.

- Listen to Peter: 'He himself bore our sins in his body on the tree' (1 Peter 2:24). The 'tree' is, of course, Peter's way of referring to the cross.
- Listen to John, as he records something of the preaching of John the Baptist: 'The next day John saw Jesus coming towards him and said, "Look, the Lamb of God, who takes away the sin of the world!"' (John 1:29).
- Listen to Paul, as he outlines the substance of his gospel message which brings reconciliation between man and God: 'God made him who had no sin to be sin for us, so that in him we might become the righteousness of God' (2 Corinthians 5:21).

We love the infancy motifs of the Christmas story, the softness of the baby in the manger. But why did the Son of God become a baby? A fundamental part of the answer is that he entered the world as a real human being, identifying himself with us, in order that he might be one with us and so be our legitimate substitute — a human being bearing human sin.

Christ's death was a penal work

We now live in a world full of cars and traffic. When you are caught on the speed camera you are penalized with 'penalty points' on your driving licence. We live in a world which loves football. When you commit a foul in the box the resulting punishment is a 'penalty kick'. We live in a world of many countries and continents. Australia was once a 'penal colony' where prisoners were sent to serve their sentence. From these simple examples we see that the word 'penal' (which is central to our second major point as we consider Isaiah 53) has to do with punishment. It has to do with punishment justly inflicted by the law on someone for their offences.

Christ's substituting himself to be the one who carried our sins was with the purpose that he should suffer the punishment we deserve for our sins, and so satisfy God's justice on our behalf. This is why we use the term 'penal substitution' to describe what Christ was doing for us as he died on the cross.

That the cross involved penal substitution is made abundantly clear in verse 5:

> But he was pierced for our transgressions,
>   he was crushed for our iniquities;
> the punishment that brought us peace was upon him,
>   and by his wounds we are healed.

Penal substitution

Again there is this dichotomy between 'he' and 'we' (or 'our' or 'us'). The principle of substitution is once again obvious. But so now is the vocabulary of punishment. We misread his agony (v. 4). Actually (v. 5), he was suffering for our sins. He was bearing the penalty which ought to have been ours.

The word 'pierced' is found in Isaiah 51:9, where it is used of the death wound inflicted on the metaphorical monster (Egypt). It usually means 'to pierce fatally'. This language makes us think of the piercing nails of the crucifixion. 'Crushed' is used of people being trampled to death, being stamped on again and again, until they die. (Christ's death was not immediate. He suffered on the cross for hours.) And these sufferings were 'for', or 'because of', our transgressions and our iniquities.

Now the point to note is that this was not a loose or an accidental 'because of' — like a child who dies 'because of' the sinful reckless driving of a drunk behind the wheel of a car. No. This 'for', or 'because of', represents a definite legal purpose. This is indicated in the second part of verse 5. It was the punishment necessary by law to secure or restore our peace — the sinner's peace with God. These death wounds of Christ were the wounds which had the purpose of bringing our healing. The clear meaning is that the sufferings of Christ were such as to satisfy justice for our sins and so bring us peace with God and at the same time restore us to true humanity.

Again we find this penal theme, the satisfying of God's justice, God's righteous wrath for our sin, echoed constantly in the New Testament.

- Romans 3:25-26 tells us: 'God presented him as a sacrifice of atonement, through faith in his blood. He did this to demonstrate his justice, because in his forbearance he had left the sins committed beforehand unpunished — he did it to demonstrate his justice at the present time, so as to be just and the one who justifies those who have faith in Jesus.' Jesus' death atoned for our sins, so that God's justice is satisfied, but at the same time we sinners are forgiven.

• Galatians 3:13 speaks in similar terms of the cross of Jesus: 'Christ redeemed us from the curse of the law by becoming a curse for us, for it is written: "Cursed is everyone who is hung on a tree."' Notice the vocabulary of law and the principle of substitution embedded in the text. Christ redeemed us from the curse by becoming a curse for us. By Jesus' death on the cross we sinners were redeemed from the curse of the law, the just condemnation we deserved for flouting God's law. Jesus operated as our penal substitute.

• For more on the principle of penal substitution in Christ's death see also Mark 10:45; Romans 4:25; 1 Corinthians 15:3-4; 2 Corinthians 5:21; Galatians 2:20; 4:4-5; Ephesians 5:25; Hebrews 9:28; 1 Peter 3:18; 1 John 3:16.

The Bible teaches that Christ's death involved penal substitution. This is at the heart of the gospel. This is not, as some would dismiss it, one 'theory' of the atonement. This is what Scripture says actually happened.

Christ's death was a divine work

God was at work at Calvary. We are told that in verse 6:

> We all, like sheep, have gone astray,
>   each of us has turned to his own way;
> and the LORD has laid on him
>   the iniquity of us all.

We self-willed wandering sheep going our own way, all going in our different directions, are each responsible for our choices, for our sins. But, by contrast, the LORD God has made all our sins and iniquities to meet together on Christ. They were laid upon him by God so that he would suffer for us and we would be justly forgiven.

Objections to the doctrine

There are two objections which those who do not like what the Scriptures teach throw up concerning penal substitution. Let us look at them.

1. How can one person's sin — what the individual is responsible for — be transferred to another person?

'It can't be done!' people say. 'When one human being is charged with committing a felony that was actually perpetrated by another person, we call that a miscarriage of justice!'

But although that is, of course, generally true, it is not quite the full picture, is it? For example, when a child or a minor does something wrong, often the law will hold the parents responsible. The parents themselves were not the ones who did wrong. Nevertheless they are held responsible. That is what all the shenanigans over truancy were about recently in Britain, in reaction to government proposals that parents should be fined for their youngsters failing to turn up at school. So, even at a human level, it's not quite true that sin and responsibility can never be legally transferred.

But, further, throughout the Old Testament God indicated the transfer of sin and guilt, as pictured in the animal sacrifices. This is explicit in the case of the scapegoat used in the sacrificial ceremonies of the Day of Atonement. We read of Aaron, the high priest, in Leviticus 16:21-22:

> He is to lay both hands on the head of the live goat and confess over it all the wickedness and rebellion of the Israelites — all their sins — and put them on the

goat's head. He shall send the goat away into the desert in the care of a man appointed for the task. The goat will carry on itself all their sins to a solitary place; and the man shall release it in the desert.

Here we have an Old Testament picture of the transfer of our sins to Christ, who carried them to the cross, that solitary place of abandonment, never to return to us again. This is the work God achieved through Christ, not simply in picture form, but in reality.

2. Isn't it simply monstrous injustice for someone to suffer for another person's sins?

Here is a second objection closely related to the first. This concerns not the *possibility* of transferring guilt, but the *justice* of such a thing. 'How could it be at all right, for example, to execute your granny for the murder you carried out?' some might object. 'That's the kind of thing a totalitarian dictator would do, not a just and loving God.'

But the answer to this objection resides in the uniqueness of who Jesus is. This objection may carry weight if Jesus were just a man, but he is not. He is the Son of God, God and man in one person (John 1:1,14: 5:18; Philippians 2:6). As God, Jesus is not some innocent third party who is frogmarched off to a kangaroo court which leads to the gallows. He is one with his Father and fully complicit in the plan of our salvation. Again, his willingness to suffer is the theme of Isaiah 53:7-9:

> He was oppressed and afflicted,
>   yet he did not open his mouth;
> he was led like a lamb to the slaughter,
>   and as a sheep before her shearers is silent,
>   so he did not open his mouth
>
>   (v. 7).

Though he is unjustly accused, he says nothing. He raises no protest.

Secondly, Jesus' substitutionary death for us would have been an injustice if his death had been the end of him. But it wasn't, and Jesus knew it wouldn't be. In John 10:17, he says, 'The reason my Father loves me is that I lay down my life — only to take it up again.' He truly and fully died for us, but he was not, as it were, robbed of the rest of his life. As a righteous man, as the Son of God, he would rise again. Again Isaiah foresaw this in his prophecy:

> ... though the LORD makes his life a guilt offering,
> he will see his offspring and prolong his days...
> After the suffering of his soul,
>   he will see the light [of life] and be satisfied
>
>   (vv. 10-11).

And, indeed, Christ himself as the victim in no way lost out by the cross, but rather his true worth — his amazing love and kindness to sinners, his true glory — was displayed to all the universe for time and eternity through what he did for us there.

The cross is gruesome and awful because our sins are gruesome and awful, but it is not unjust. The cross is the work of God, and as such is carried out with perfect justice and integrity, and that means that with perfect justice and integrity God can forgive sinners like you and me. We are to understand, believe, worship and adore!

A 'DONE' DEAL

As we have already noticed, later in verse 11 of Isaiah's wonderful fifty-third chapter, which so marvellously predicts the sufferings of Calvary, we read of Jesus, 'After the suffering of his soul, he will see the light [of life] and be satisfied.'

The suffering of Christ's soul we take to be his death on the cross. Therefore the fact that after that 'he will see the light of life' is prophetic of the resurrection of Christ. Furthermore, the resurrection here is linked with Christ's being 'satisfied'. The resurrection indicates that Christ's death, the penal substitution atoning for our sins, was a completed work. If a job is only half done, we cannot rest satisfied. We feel as though we need to get on and finish it off. But what Jesus achieved by his death on the cross required nothing to be added to it. Indeed, his dying words included the great cry from the cross, 'It is finished' (John 19:30). Through his substitutionary death the sins of all who believe have been thoroughly dealt with and their salvation is secure. It is a 'done deal' in which Christ can rest satisfied.

I have always liked the way that Donald Grey Barnhouse, an American preacher of the mid-twentieth century, explained the connection between the cross and the resurrection:

> Every one of us at some time or other has walked into some office to pay a bill, perhaps for telephone service or electricity... We handed the money to the teller who was appointed to act for the company to whom we were indebted. The teller counted our money ... and handed us a receipt. The company could never collect that bill from us again. If they tried to do so, we could produce the receipt and they would know that the matter had been cleared, and that we were free from the obligation for ever. The Lord Jesus walked up to Calvary, which was God's desk for the payment of our sins. The account was heavy against us, and the Lord Jesus Christ could settle the account only by shedding his blood in dying for us... He offered up his life, and God the Father took that life, handed it over to his justice for execution, while his holiness turned away from the scene, leaving the Saviour alone

to cry out, 'My God! My God! Why have you forsaken me?' (Matthew 27:46). When the three hours of daylight and the three hours of darkness were ended, the payment had been made in full. Those hours were eternal as far as God was concerned... They took that body and reverently cared for it, putting it in the tomb, wrapping it in linen with myrrh that was the symbol of death. But it was not possible that the Lord Jesus should be holden by death at this point. He had paid the complete debt, and the Lord God Almighty reached out, as a cashier might stamp a bill paid in full, and raised his Son Jesus Christ from the dead, as the sign that there was nothing more to pay... He paid it all, and the resurrection is the receipt for the bill.[2]

Christ's suffering and death are the payment for sin; the resurrection is the receipt confirming that there is nothing left to pay. That is why Isaiah explains that after his death Jesus would 'see the light of life and be satisfied'.

In the substitutionary death of Christ, God's justice is completely satisfied once and for all, and this in such a way that all believing sinners are completely forgiven. Is God a God who ignores the claims of justice in order to forgive? Absolutely not. The cross assures us not only that there is ultimate justice in the universe, but also that there is forgiveness for all who trust in Christ crucified. The truth of the death of Jesus as a penal substitution could not be more important.

EVIDENCE

There is one obvious final point to make, which is always worth reasserting.

As we noted at the beginning of our exposition, Isaiah was writing some time before 700 BC. This passage prophesies the sufferings and the resurrection of Christ in minute detail, even down to his being condemned along with criminals (v. 12) and being laid in a rich man's tomb (v. 9; cf. Luke 23:32-33; Matthew 27:57-60). If you want evidence of the reality of God and the truth of the gospel, here it is. It is fashionable these days for secular critics to caricature Christian faith as a total leap in the dark, a belief despite evidence to the contrary. Actually nothing could be further from the truth. We believe because of the evidence, not contrary to it.

How do we know there is an eternal God who knows the end from the beginning? Where is the evidence? Well, here is a very large slice of evidence, right in front of our eyes in the verses of Isaiah chapter 53. No mere human being could possibly have predicted with such accuracy what would happen to Jesus 700 years in advance. Isaiah 53 is only possible because the living God, who stands above time, revealed these things to his servant Isaiah.

What's the big deal for me?

This chapter has taught us that Christ has died for our sins, and so a Christian never need feel condemned.

An incident from the life of the nineteenth-century Irish evangelist Brownlow North[3] serves to show us the power of what this can mean in our personal lives. As a member of the Irish aristocracy, in his younger life, before his conversion, he had indulged in all the sins to which rich young men are prone. Now he was a Christian and was preaching the gospel to large crowds and packed churches.

One evening when Brownlow North was about to enter the vestry of a church in which he was due to preach, a stranger came up to him and said, 'Here is a letter for you of great importance, and you are requested to read it before you preach tonight.' Thinking it might be from someone in need of prayer, he immediately opened it. To his shock he found that it was a letter spelling out in some detail his past sins. It concluded with words to this effect: 'How dare you, being conscious of the truth of all the above, pray and speak to people about their souls this evening, when you are such a vile sinner?' His past was being used to accuse him, and he was being charged with being a terrible hypocrite.

Brownlow North put the letter in his pocket, entered the pulpit and, after he had prayed, addressed the congregation. What did he say? He produced the letter and informed the people of all its contents. But then he went on: 'All that is said here is true, and it is a correct picture of the degraded sinner that I once was; and oh how wonderful must the grace be that could quicken and raise me up from such a death in trespasses and sins, and make me what I appear before you tonight ... one who knows that all his past sins have been cleansed away through the atoning blood of the Lamb of God. It is of his redeeming love that I have now to tell you, and to entreat any here who are not yet reconciled to God to come this night to Jesus, that he may take their sins away and heal them.' His hearers were deeply impressed by his honesty and his testimony to the love of Christ, the one on whom all our sins were laid and carried away into oblivion, never to be seen again.

The letter which had been intended to silence the preacher and cover him in confusion actually became the means of opening many hearts as they saw in Brownlow North the truth of the statement that 'There is now no condemnation for those who are in Christ Jesus' (Romans 8:1).

Our sins have been paid for by the blood of Christ. We need never feel condemned. We can be honest about our darkest failures, past and present, with the great assurance that God still loves us and accepts us. 'If we claim to be without sin, we deceive ourselves and the truth is not in us. If we confess our sins, he is faithful and just and will forgive us our sins and purify us from all unrighteousness' (1 John 1:8-9).

What a tremendous relief it is as we grasp this truth! It leads us to thank God and praise his name for such mercy and kindness.

Big deal 3
Justification — right with God

ROMANS 3:21-26

> But now a righteousness from God, apart from law, has been made known, to which the Law and the Prophets testify. This righteousness from God comes through faith in Jesus Christ to all who believe. There is no difference, for all have sinned and fall short of the glory of God, and are justified freely by his grace through the redemption that came by Christ Jesus. God presented him as a sacrifice of atonement, through faith in his blood. He did this to demonstrate his justice, because in his forbearance he had left the sins committed beforehand unpunished — he did it to demonstrate his justice at the present time, so as to be just and the one who justifies those who have faith in Jesus.

How does a person — a sinful person like you or me — get right with God? The answer is found in Romans 3:26. God 'justifies' us. This is what the cross enables God to do: 'God presented him as a sacrifice of atonement ... so as to be just and the one who justifies those who have faith in Jesus.'

In this chapter we return to Romans 3 and we look more fully at this wonderful truth of justification. It is impossible to overemphasize how important it is. It is such a big deal that if we tamper with the gospel at this point the apostle Paul said our good news becomes bad news; it becomes another gospel which is not a gospel at all (Galatians 1:6-7).

Martin Luther understood this, telling us, 'If the article of justification be once lost, then all true Christian doctrine is lost.' It's 'game over' for the church, and for Christians, if we get this wrong.

But on the other hand, if we grasp and hold on to the Bible's teaching about justification we will find it a vast source of joy and assurance.

THE MEANING OF JUSTIFICATION

This is where clarity is vital, so let me begin by explaining two things which justification is not and then clarifying what it actually is.

1. Do not confuse justification and sanctification

These are two completely separate things. Sanctification is concerned with a person's character, their moral and spiritual quality. But justification is not about a person's character — it is about their status in the eyes of God's law.

There are other differences. Sanctification is a process in which the Holy Spirit changes us as people and makes us holy. But justification is not a process, but a once-for-all event whereby a person is declared righteous by God.

We tend to confuse these two things, but we must not. We confuse them because naturally (under the influence of our cynical and sinful hearts) we don't believe the good news. We are inclined to think people get right with God by their own merits — how holy and pleasing to God they have become in character. This is going back to that 'Churchianity' we ran into at the outset of the book. But that is not the gospel. Rather, the strange and wonderful good news is that God justifies people who are not righteous in themselves. The apostle Paul is so bold as to declare in Romans 4:5 that we should trust 'God who justifies the wicked'. Shock horror! But that is the wonder of the gospel.

2. Do not confuse justification and adoption, or inclusion in God's family

Granted, both of these are changes of status which are true of Christians and are obviously very closely linked to justification, but they are distinct.

'Justification' is not a relational word. It is not about 'How am I linked with this person?' or whether or not I am included in this or that group. Rather it is a forensic word, a word from a court of law. In the Greek of the New Testament it is related to a whole category of words with the stem '*dik*' which relate to the category of the law. In secular Greek a *dikasta* is a judge, a *dikaniko* is a lawyer, a *dike* is a trial. In the Greek of the New Testament itself *dikaiōma* is a regulation or commandment, *dikaiōs* is an adverb which means that something is done justly, *dikaiosune* is righteousness (being right before the law), *adikia* is the opposite (wrongdoing); and *dikaioō* is to justify, to declare righteous (see Romans 3:20). Understandably once God declares us righteous we enter his family — we are adopted by him. How could God not own those who are righteous? But the two things are separate.

New Perspective theologians are currently trying to change the idea behind justification to persuade us that it has more to do with inclusion. This development, whether consciously or unconsciously, seems driven by an agenda to make the gospel more acceptable to Western society's prevailing culture. There are three things involved.

- First, this plays better with the 'touchy/feely' relational outlook of our postmodern society, whereas 'law', with its obligations and standards to which all are held accountable, is a turn-off for many contemporary Westerners (though not, we have to say, for other cultures).

- Secondly, since differences over justification lay at the heart of the Reformation division between Protestants and Catholics, this shift in the meaning of justification has an ecumenical edge to it. It makes it look as though there is really no problem and Protestants and Catholics should simply reunite. This plays well in a secular society which believes that all religion should be put in one box and equates any statement of religious differences with intolerance.
- Thirdly, this move reflects the current church's doubts about Genesis 1 – 3 concerning the creation and the historical fall of mankind into sin. The gospel for the New Perspective theologians inclines towards taking the covenant with Abraham in Genesis 12, with God's promise of blessing and inclusion for the nations through Abraham's seed, as its starting point. I don't dispute that the covenant with Abraham is central to the gospel. But actually the roots of the gospel go much further back — to Adam. That means that the blessing promised to Abraham must be seen in the larger context of the curse on Adam and his descendants for sin — that is, their lack of righteousness. And, for those who know their Bibles, I will just make the point that it is there, with Adam, that Paul begins his great explanation of the gospel in Romans 1 and anchors his summary of the gospel in the latter half of Romans 5.

So I would encourage readers not to be taken in by this New Perspective tampering with justification.

Having cleared away those confusions, we can now move on to a definition of what justification actually is.

3. Justification is the declaration of the judge that a person is right in the eyes of the law

We begin by simply looking at the meaning of the word 'justify'. As we have already shown from its Greek stem *dik*, it is a word from a legal background, and there are two simple ways of clarifying its biblical use.

First, consider *the use of the verb 'to justify' in Luke 7:29*. The context is that John the Baptist, in prison and under pressure, had sent some of his disciples to ask Jesus for confirmation that he was the Christ. Jesus replied by pointing to the miracles he was performing, which were his credentials as the Christ. He then went on to affirm the ministry of John the Baptist as being from God — something about which the religious authorities were ambivalent. But, by contrast with the religious leaders, we read, 'All the people, even the tax collectors, when they heard Jesus' words, acknowledged that God's way was right [literally, "justified God"] because they had been baptized by John.' We can see the meaning of the word 'justify' from the way the NIV translates it — 'acknowledged God's way was right'. Leon Morris explains the verse with great clarity. He says, 'These common people justified God. This means they "pronounced God just", they accepted the ways of God as they truly were and did not try to constrain him into a mould of their own manufacture.'[1]

In contrast to the New Perspective view of justification, the common people were certainly not pronouncing God as being included in something. In contrast to a classical Roman Catholic view of justification, it is impossible that they were somehow making God's character more holy. No. What they were doing was to declare that God's way (as seen in the ministry of John the Baptist) was right. This is what justification means.

Secondly, that 'to justify' means to declare someone to be righteous, or 'in the right', is seen from the fact that *the word is used as the opposite of the idea of condemnation.* For example, look at Deuteronomy 25:1. The Septuagint, the Greek version of the Old Testament, uses the word *dikaiŏō*. The verse reads, 'When men have a dispute, they are to take it to court and the judges will decide the case, acquitting [or justifying] the innocent and condemning the guilty.' To justify, or to acquit, is the opposite of the judges condemning something.

We find the same when we read Romans 8:33-34: 'Who will bring any charge against those whom God has chosen? It is God who justifies. Who is he that condemns?' Again the Greek is the verb *dikaiŏō*, and the context is a law-court setting, with charges being brought. Here, as we have seen before, 'to justify' is the opposite of 'to condemn'. So when the judge declares a defendant guilty, what he is doing is condemning him. But when the judge declares the defendant acquitted, not guilty, right before the law, what he is doing is 'justifying' him. Justification does not change the person himself. The individual in the dock is the same person in himself two seconds after the judge speaks as he was two seconds before the judge spoke. But what has changed is his status.

Such a change of status in the eyes of the law makes all the difference in the world to someone. Think about it in terms of mere national law. The defendant will not go to prison. There is nothing against the justified man's name. He exits the courtroom right before the law. Nothing has to go on his CV when he applies for jobs, or for car insurance, or whatever; he has a clean status.

Justification is a change of status for the sinner — from being under suspicion, or guilty, to being counted not guilty and in the right. It is the change from being the just object of God's condemnation, and therefore of his wrath for our sins, to being right with God.

Justification includes two things. The first is *the forgiveness of all our sins by God* — a cancelling of all the debts we owe, or will ever owe, to God's law.

Secondly, *we are declared righteous in God's sight*. We are not forgiven yet still deemed guilty — as if the offended party simply refused to press charges. God does not say, 'Guilty but forgiven'; he says, 'Not guilty'. In fact he says more than that. He declares us positively righteous and pleasing to himself — not just neutral, as though we had never done anything wrong, but righteous, as though we had lived our whole lives in a way that positively pleased the all-holy God. It is truly curious and completely unexpected that God should do such a thing for people like us. But that is what justification means.

What a blessing! Who would be without it? So, if you are asking, 'How can I get right with God?' understand that what you need is not to try harder, but to be justified. It's not about what you need to do for yourself, but about what God can do for you — justification.

THE GROUND OF JUSTIFICATION

The astonishing truth of the gospel is that God does this for sinners, for people who don't deserve it. He acquits bad characters. He justifies the wicked.

On what grounds, on what basis, can God do this? In the Old Testament Proverbs 17:15 says that the judge who acquits the guilty is detestable in the Lord's sight. Yet this is what God does. What right does he have to do this? And, just to intensify the paradox, look again at Romans 3:26: 'He did it to demonstrate his justice at the present time, so as to be just and the one who justifies those who have faith in Jesus.' God justifies sinners, and this verse says that God is just when he does it! He is perfectly entitled to do it. There is no fudge, no sleight of hand. How can that be?

In Christ

The logic is in that phrase in verse 24, 'by', or 'in Christ Jesus'. It is 'in Christ Jesus' that God can do this remarkable thing. We find the same emphasis echoed in Romans 8:1: 'There is now no condemnation for those who are in Christ Jesus.' That phrase, 'in Christ', which permeates the whole New Testament, is where the whole rationale of justification resides. Here is God's right to do this astonishing thing of declaring sinners righteous. Here is the ground for justification.

Certain environments enable you to do things that are impossible elsewhere. For example, in a hothouse environment it is possible to grow flowers and fruit which just would not grow in the colder climate outside. Or again, in a sterile environment surgeons are able to perform complicated operations on needy patients without the risk of infection entering the wound that there would otherwise be.

But perhaps the most striking example of the consequences produced by a change of environment comes in space. Though on earth our bodies will always weigh something, and so our movements will be restricted to some extent, in space almost the very opposite applies. We can experience what it is to be weightless. Though on earth we might tip the scales in a big way, in space we would be lighter than a feather. The effects of gravity have been neutralized. Here is not the place to go into the physics of all this, but astronauts can literally fly around the inside of their space capsule. The new environment has changed everything.

In just the same way, though in the environment of being under God's law we are guilty sinners, if, through faith, we are 'in Christ', we are nevertheless legitimately declared righteous. The change of environment has made the impossible possible.

The great exchange

The New Testament confronts us with a mysterious exchange which takes place for those 'in Christ'. We touched on it in the last chapter when we considered Isaiah 53: 'He was pierced for our transgressions.' On the cross the sins of those in Christ, including all their particularity and depth of wickedness, were reckoned to Christ. And there at Calvary's cross, as our substitute, he bears the just punishment for our sin completely. He is treated as the worst sinner deserves — the worst adulterer, the worst liar, the worst murderer, the worst blasphemer, etc. He bears the full impassioned torrent of the righteous wrath of God which our sins deserve. 'God presented him as a sacrifice of atonement' (Romans 3:25). The word translated 'sacrifice of atonement' is more literally 'propitiation' — that which appeases God's righteous anger. There the just wrath of God is expended on Christ and decisively quenched for sin, once and for all.

However, there is another consideration to bear in mind. At the same time as he pays for our sins, Christ goes to the cross out of obedience to God. Philippians 2:8 tells us that, 'Being found in appearance as a man, [Jesus] humbled himself and became obedient to death — even death on a cross.' He obeyed God, his Father, to the uttermost. This obedience of Christ also pertains to our salvation. The second part of the great exchange is that the righteous life of Christ is reckoned by God to us who are in Christ. Of Jesus, God the Father said, 'This is my Son, whom I love; with him I am well pleased.' And in Christ, that 'well pleased' is now said of us!

What is more, the righteousness counted to those in Christ is none other than a righteousness 'from God' (Romans 3:21-22) and, indeed, as we shall see in a later chapter, can legitimately be called 'the righteousness of God'. By this mysterious exchange, by the unspeakable grace of God, I (a sinner) stand before God in the righteousness of God! And that means it is impossible for God to find fault with it, for if he did he would be finding fault with himself.

Note what Paul says in 2 Corinthians 5:21: 'God made him who had no sin to be sin for us, so that in him we might become the righteousness of God.'

Notice the 'in him'. Our sins are conferred on Christ and his righteousness conferred on us, so our right standing, our acceptance with God, is positively guaranteed. We will open up 2 Corinthians 5:21 further in the next chapter. But the point to notice is that it all happens 'in Christ'. In this new environment everything changes for us. Sinners are counted righteous. This is the gospel! Martin Luther, sitting in a tower in Wittenberg, was meditating on Romans when the truth of all this dawned on him. He wrote, 'When I realized this I felt myself absolutely born again. The gates of paradise had been flung open and I had entered. There and then the whole of Scripture took on another look to me.'

How can God justify? How can he declare sinful people righteous? 'In Christ Jesus'. There is the answer. There is the ground of justification.

But, of course, it is ours only as we are 'in Christ'. It is of no avail to us until we are 'in Christ'. Positively it is ours by incorporation into him. So how is this appropriated? How are we joined to Jesus?

THE INSTRUMENT OF JUSTIFICATION

What does God require of us in order that we should be justified? The answer (taking us back to chapter 1, of course) is faith. It is by faith that we are placed 'in Christ', or joined to Christ, and so justified. Faith is the instrument because faith unites us to him. Paul says, 'This righteousness from God comes through faith in Jesus Christ to all who believe' (Romans 3:22). We have looked at this before in chapter 1, but let me emphasize five things briefly.

1. Faith is not meritorious

Faith is not itself our righteousness. It is not as if God says, 'Well, they have messed up on keeping my commands, but instead of that I'll accept their faith as meriting acceptance with me.' No. It is not our faith which is our righteousness, but Christ who is our righteousness (1 Corinthians 1:30). We are not justified 'on account of faith', but 'by means of faith'. Faith is how Christ becomes ours, and so his righteousness becomes ours. Its function is not to deserve or merit, but simply to unite us to Christ, or place us 'in Christ'. And we find that Jesus is more than willing to receive sinners. He calls us to 'come' to him (Matthew 11:28). He is more than willing to have sinners joined to him. We see this in the Gospels as he allowed many sick people to touch him and be healed (Mark 5:25-34).

2. Faith in what?

It is faith in Jesus Christ. He is the object of our faith. It is not (Hollywood style) faith in faith — 'If I believe hard enough I will be saved.' This is to think that faith itself is the power that saves. It is not. Salvation is in Jesus Christ. Do not look at your faith. That way leads to subjectivism and spiritual depression. Look at Christ; look to Jesus! Also notice something else here. You are not invited to believe that you are saved, and if you believe that then you are saved. That is to confuse faith with assurance. We are to trust in Christ. 'I believe' = 'I believe Christ is able to save sinners and I personally put my trust in him to save me and commit my soul to Jesus Christ, the Son of God.'

3. Faith alone

Here again we are reminded of what we saw in chapter 1. It is not faith in Christ plus something. It is not faith in Christ plus keeping God's law, or being good, or growth in grace, or church attendance, or receiving the sacraments, or anything else. It is (as the Americans would say) simply faith in Christ, period. The wise Dr Lloyd-Jones said that because it is faith alone, the true gospel is so free that it will always lay itself open to the charge Paul faced in Romans 6: 'If what you are saying is right, why not continue in sin that grace may abound?' That objection can only arise if justification has nothing at all to do with works. And that was what Paul was accused of because he preached that justification is by faith alone. There is no argument of internal logic against the charge, only a spiritual argument: 'I cannot go on in sin, because I now belong to Jesus and his kingdom.'

4. No one can believe in Christ too soon

People are inclined to put it off: 'When should I believe?' The answer is, the very moment you need justification. When is that moment? It is now. 'Now is the time of God's favour, now is the day of salvation' (2 Corinthians 6:2).

5. Faith means that a Christian is permanently right with God

True faith in Christ means that because of his cross all our sins, past, present and future, are dealt with. We are permanently right with God. Martin Luther comments on this matter as follows, using an illustration from family life:

> But here one may say: the sins which we daily commit offend and anger God; how then can we be holy? Answer: A mother's love to her child is much stronger than the distaste of the scurf upon the child's head. Even so, God's love towards us is far stronger than our uncleanness. Therefore, though we be sinners, yet we lose not thereby our childhood, neither do we fall from grace by reason of our sins.

How can sinners like you and me get right with God? The answer is, through being justified in Christ. The meaning of justification is to be declared righteous by God. The ground of justification, the basis on which God can do this, is 'in Christ'. The instrument of justification, that which makes justification ours, is faith in Jesus Christ.

What's the big deal for me?

This great truth of justification which we have thought about in this chapter teaches us that Christ has done everything needed to put believers right with God.

Many Christians believe this, but it does not make the impact on their lives that it should. They believe it in their heads, but do not feel it in their hearts.

Mandy is someone who was brought up in quite a strict Christian family. In many ways that was a great blessing to her. But there were many rules and regulations. For example, the children were never allowed to play out of doors on a Sunday. Also the family always ate roast dinner on Saturday night so that there would not be too much washing up to do on the Lord's Day. Other Christians who were less strict in these matters were looked upon with disapproval. Finding this atmosphere irksome, even after she became a Christian, Mandy was always left feeling guilty as a result of the well-meant rules of the house. She might be a Christian, but not a very good one.

When she was grown up and married to Dave, Mandy worked caring for the elderly. She was in fact terrific at her job, very friendly and someone who made older people feel much loved. But, being a sensitive girl and knowing how very precious human beings are to God, she was acutely aware of how much better service she would have liked to give to her patients. She fell short of the high standards she set herself and would constantly 'beat herself up' mentally. 'I fail all the time,' she told herself.

And it was the same when it came to church and Christian faith. Her husband, Dave, came from a family who had always been high-profile Christians, eager to witness to others or take on responsibilities at church. Mandy wasn't like that. She was a fairly retiring kind of personality. Once again, though she trusted the Lord Jesus Christ, it was an area of her life in which she felt a failure. 'Dave will get straight into heaven when he dies,' she was heard to say, 'but I'm not sure God will want a loser like me.'

Mandy's Christian life was blighted because, although she trusted in Christ alone as her Lord and Saviour, she still had not grasped the enormity of what Christ has done for his people. Instead of living on her feelings of inadequacy, Mandy needed to live by faith in the completed work of Christ, who takes our sins away and, whatever our failures, makes us totally acceptable to God.

If you are like Mandy, it would be good for you to reread this chapter on justification, praying that the Holy Spirit will help you to understand deep in your heart the truth of justification by faith.

Big deal 4
Imputed righteousness — a legal fiction?

2 Corinthians 5:17-21

Therefore, if anyone is in Christ, he is a new creation; the old has gone, the new has come! All this is from God, who reconciled us to himself through Christ and gave us the ministry of reconciliation: that God was reconciling the world to himself in Christ, not counting men's sins against them. And he has committed to us the message of reconciliation. We are therefore Christ's ambassadors, as though God were making his appeal through us. We implore you on Christ's behalf: Be reconciled to God. God made him who had no sin to be sin for us, so that in him we might become the righteousness of God.

Is there a hope of heaven right up to the very last breath of this life? Is there any point in turning to Christ at such a time, or have many people already blown their chances by then?

There he was, a bad man — in human terms a man almost certainly far worse than any reader of this book. He had threatened and robbed and murdered, and now the authorities were executing him. It was the end. He was at death's door. He had been bad all his life and there was no time to change things now. 'Is it too late?' he thought. 'Is there any hope for people like me at this last minute?'

It's quite a question, isn't it? And it isn't one that is relevant only at a personal level. This is something that Christians think about with reference to others, especially as they see elderly unbelieving relatives or friends coming towards the end of this life. Is there any use in speaking to them of Jesus in their last hours, or is it too late?

But the wonderful answer of the gospel to the question, 'Is there any hope at death's door?' is a resounding 'Yes!' Isn't that wonderful? The crucified Jesus said to that bad man, the dying thief on the adjacent cross who asked him for help, 'I tell you the truth, today you will be with me in paradise' (Luke 23:43). That is the gospel. That is its power. It can save anyone, right up to the last possible moment.

How can God do that?

How is this possible? We have to keep asking questions like that in this book as we contemplate the wonderful things God does for sinners. How can God do what the New Testament says he does — 'justify the wicked' as they turn to Christ in faith? It is possible because of the marvellous truth of 'imputed righteousness'. This is a subject we need to consider next in following through on the last chapter about justification. This is the second part of that great exchange which we mentioned there. We are now going to focus more closely on that.

When God justifies sinners — that is, declares us righteous through faith in Christ — he is not fudging things. Not only does God declare us righteous, but he constitutes the very state which he declares to be true. He not only proclaims us righteous, but he establishes that as the case. He does so by imputing Christ's righteousness to us who believe — in other words, he regards Christ's righteousness as belonging to us; he reckons it, or credits it, to our account. He is able to do that legitimately because we are one with Jesus through faith in him; we are 'in Christ'.

Now there are some people who find this impossible to believe. In fact they object to it and try to rubbish it. One of the New Perspective theologians has opposed this doctrine. He has written, thinking of God as our judge, '"Righteousness" is not a quality or a substance that can be transferred from the judge to the defendant.' He is saying that righteousness is not something you can just give to someone as if it were a bar of chocolate or a sack of potatoes. He thinks it is not something like money which you can easily transfer from one bank account to another. Therefore he concludes that it can't be done. At first his argument sounds persuasive. We think to ourselves that most things that we give each other are material objects, and righteousness is not something material. 'Perhaps the critic is right,' we are tempted to think. 'How can this so-called imputed righteousness make any sense?'

LEGAL STATUS

But actually this objection relies on a kind of sleight of hand. The doctrine of imputation does not look upon righteousness as a 'quality' or 'substance' that is passed from one to another, and it never has done. It sees it first of all as a legal status. And, of course, there are many examples in which a legal status of one sort or another is given to, or conferred on, people by a judge or by someone else in authority. These things are not 'legal fictions'. They are totally legitimate.

- Think of *adoption*. The courts confer the status of 'family member' on the child. In the eyes of the law that child is now part of the family.
- Think of *marriage*. The registrar confers the marital status on the husband and wife as a consequence of the marriage ceremony. In the eyes of the law those two people are now Mr and Mrs Smith.

IMPUTED RIGHTEOUSNESS

- Think of *acquittal*. The defendant has been on trial, but now the judge declares that person not guilty. He or she is reckoned to be 'right' before the law.
- Think of *diplomatic immunity*. The government confers that status on the staff of another country's embassy. They are considered not liable to lawsuit or prosecution under the laws of the host country.

It is just like this when God imputes righteousness to believers. He reckons a new legal status of righteousness to belong to them. This is a free gift from God to all who believe. That is how there is hope for sinful people even at death's door. God will confer the status of being right with him on all who believe — even at the last moment.

In 2 Corinthians 5:19-21 we have a classic New Testament statement of the truth of imputed righteousness. I want to do two things in tandem with this passage, particularly focusing on verse 21. I want to explain the text, and I want to do so drawing on a number of other Bible passages to show that the good news of imputed righteousness is not a sideshow, but has a central place in our salvation; in other words, it is a big deal. It is a theme which runs right through Scripture.

2 Corinthians 5:21 tells us, 'God made him who had no sin to be sin for us, so that in him we might become the righteousness of God.' I love this verse because it begins and ends with God! There are basically four matters here: first, the sinlessness of Christ; second, the imputing of our sins to Christ; third, the imputing of his righteousness to us; fourth, (implicitly) our being reconciled to God.

THE SINLESSNESS OF CHRIST

Verse 21 begins, 'God made him who had no sin...' The 'him' here is Jesus. Christ's sinlessness uniquely qualified him to carry our sins and to confer on us his righteousness. Christ is a most mysterious and wonderful person. He is both God and man. In his divine nature he could know no sin. In his human nature there was not the least taint of sin even though he had been tested and tempted by Satan himself. His disciples knew he was sinless. Peter declared, 'He committed no sin' (1 Peter 2:22). The apostle John wrote, 'And in him is no sin' (1 John 3:5). The writer to the Hebrews told his readers that Jesus was 'tempted in every way, just as we are — yet was without sin' (Hebrews 4:15). Even his earthly judge, Pontius Pilate, said, 'I find no fault in him at all' (John 18:38, NKJV). Here is Jesus (in the terms of 1 Peter), the sacrificial lamb without blemish or defect.

Where does this truth of imputed righteousness begin in Scripture? It starts right back in Genesis 3 with an innocent ('sinless') animal. Adam and Eve had fallen into sin and had come under God's subsequent curse, which included physical death and being barred from the tree of life. But at the same time God announced his gracious plan of salvation through Christ.

Clothing Adam and Eve

In Genesis 3:15 God warned Satan that his head would be crushed by the seed of the woman — the Messiah, the Christ. But in Genesis 3:21 God proclaimed Christ to Adam and Eve. He did this by way of an action rather than words: 'The LORD God made garments of skin for Adam and his wife and clothed them' (Genesis 3:21). As they fell into sin they became ashamed of their nakedness. Sin had contaminated their innocence. They tried to cover up with fig leaves, which proved totally inadequate. But God covered their guilt properly and effectively with the skin of an innocent substitute. Here was an animal (was it a lamb?) which had not participated in Adam and Eve's disobedience, but none the less paid sin's penalty of death, and Adam and

Eve, who did not share the animal's innocence, none the less were clothed by it so as to stand acceptable in God's sight. We have here, in picture form, a witness to the truth of imputed righteousness. The innocent sacrifice clothed the sinners.

But this marvellous incident in the Garden of Eden is more than just a witness to the fact of imputed righteousness. Coming right at the beginning of the Bible story, it shows the central place of being clothed, the central place that imputed righteousness has in the salvation God offers us. God's first and immediate response to the Fall was an act which pictured not just Christ's sacrifice, but his righteousness being counted ours — clothing sinners. That ought to be a sign to us of how important imputed righteousness is. This is a big deal. The sinless one is the one who clothes us. From here on in, the idea of God clothing people begins to run through the Bible's pages and to have a special significance in Scripture.

The imputing of our sin to Christ

Verse 21 of 2 Corinthians 5 continues, 'God made him who had no sin to be sin for us...' God did not make Jesus a sinner. But he did make him to 'be sin'. What does that mean? We get help with this from the context. Verse 19 tells us, 'God was reconciling the world to himself in Christ, not counting men's sins against them.' He was not counting our sins against us; so what was he doing with them? It is legitimate to infer that he was counting them against Jesus. He was reckoning, or imputing, them to Christ. That is how Christ was made sin for us. God did not make Jesus a sinner, but he conferred on him the legal status of a sinner.

We have noted before, in chapter 2, that the great Old Testament picture of the transference of sin is that of the high priest laying his hands on the head of the sacrifice and so 'putting the sins' of the people on the animal (Leviticus

1:4). Of the Day of Atonement we read that the scapegoat 'will carry on itself all their sins to a solitary place' (Leviticus 16:22). The Old Testament sacrifices could not really deal with sin because they were animals which could not in fact act as substitutes for human beings (Hebrews 10:4), but they were shadows of the reality which would come in Christ. The scapegoat carrying on itself Israel's sins is the foreshadowing of our sins being transferred, imputed, to Christ and him carrying them away by dying in our place on the cross to make atonement.

Aaron's garments

As we think of the priest's work in the Old Testament, the theme of being clothed in order to be fit for God comes through again. If the priest, especially the high priest, was to deal with sin, then he himself had to be clean in God's sight. After all, he had to enter into the Most Holy Place in the tabernacle where the presence of God himself in Shekinah glory was known. Much space is devoted to the garments made for Aaron, the first high priest, in Exodus 28. The significance of these special rich garments is explained by an inscription on a gold plate worn on the high priest's head. It said, 'Holy to the LORD' (Exodus 28:36). We are told of this plate, 'It will be on Aaron's forehead continually so that they [the offerings to God through Aaron] will be acceptable to the LORD' (Exodus 28:38). The clothes which God prescribed were essential for making the high priest's work acceptable to the Lord.

The significance of the priestly clothing is brought out later in Scripture in Psalm 132. Here the priest's clothing is explicitly linked to righteousness and salvation. As the psalmist appeals to God for the fulfilment of his promises to David in the establishment of David's kingdom to the glory of God and the joy of his people, he asks God, 'May your priests be clothed with righteousness; may your saints sing

IMPUTED RIGHTEOUSNESS

for joy' (Psalm 132:9). Later in the psalm we find God responding, 'I will clothe her priests with salvation, and her saints shall ever sing for joy' (Psalm 132:16). See the parallel here between righteousness and salvation. This clothing with righteousness seems in the context to be in terms of the priests being enabled to perform their duties for the people in a legitimate manner, rather than a reference to their own personal salvation. But probably it is not possible to separate those two things. Both are in view. In any case, whatever the purpose, the point to notice is that God does clothe people in righteousness. He gives righteousness to his people.

Joshua's garments

We are led to find another bold picture of the doctrine of imputation in the vision of Zechariah 3.

What is referred to here takes place long after the initiation of the role of high priest with Aaron. With Zechariah we are now in the times just following the exile rather than those following the Exodus. A man called Joshua (not to be confused with Moses' assistant who led Israel into the promised land) is the high priest. Representing all of Israel, in the vision of Zechariah Joshua stands before the angel of the LORD in filthy clothes. The dirty garments represent the nation's sin. At his side Satan stands to accuse him. But the Lord rebukes the devil, reminding him of God's saving grace. Then we read in Zechariah 3:3-5:

> Now Joshua was dressed in filthy clothes as he stood before the angel. The angel said to those who were standing before him, 'Take off his filthy clothes.'
> Then he said to Joshua, 'See, I have taken away your sin, and I will put rich garments on you.'
> Then I said [this is Zechariah giving input into the vision], 'Put a clean turban on his head.' So they put a

clean turban on his head and clothed him, while the angel of the LORD stood by.

Not only are his filthy clothes removed, but he is clothed in rich garments. If the removal of his filthy clothes represented the removal of his sin, as the angel said, then dressing him in clean robes must mean nothing less than clothing him with righteousness. This is another intriguing picture foreshadowing what Jesus offers us by his cross; he takes our sins onto himself, but, beyond that, he places his own righteousness onto us! We have already begun to touch on the subject of our next heading.

THE IMPUTING OF CHRIST'S RIGHTEOUSNESS TO US

The whole of 2 Corinthians 5:21 reads: 'God made him who had no sin to be sin for us, so that in him we might become the righteousness of God.'

Here we note that in this verse there is a parallel between Christ's being made sin for us and our being made the righteousness of God in him. As we have already seen, when Paul says that Christ was 'made sin' he cannot mean that Christ personally became a sinner — that would have totally torpedoed the atonement made at the cross; he would then have had to pay for his own sins rather than ours. No, instead, Jesus received our sins by imputation. Our sins were reckoned his.

Now, if Jesus receives our sins by imputation, then, to keep the parallel, we receive his righteousness by imputation. The Christian does not become immediately perfect in character and behaviour any more than Christ became a sinner (with the sinful character that would have entailed). But we are given the legal status of righteousness. Just as the guilt of our sin was imputed to Christ so that he could bear it on the cross, likewise his righteousness was imputed, or credited, to us, so that we might enter into the blessing of eternal life and acceptance with a holy God.

Some people demur from this understanding of our verse. They have a fixed agenda that the expression 'the righteousness of God' is to do with God's covenant faithfulness and they seek to contort the verse into somehow accommodating that. But, though God is undoubtedly righteous in his covenant faithfulness, that cannot be its one and only meaning. The meaning of the expression 'the righteousness of God' must be allowed to be determined by the context. In this context, it must be that which does not merely undergird the general process of reconciliation (as God's faithfulness would), but it must be that which may be reckoned to us and which effects our reconciliation to God. This points clearly to the imputed righteousness of Christ.

Christ and God

Some people quibble. They say, 'Paul doesn't speak of Christ's righteousness here; rather, he speaks of the righteousness of God. You must have got it wrong.' But that is to rip things out of context. Everything that God is said to be doing in this passage is 'in Christ'. Paul has said, 'God was reconciling the world to himself in Christ' (v. 19). So here, whatever God works for us, he works through and in Christ. God was in Christ; Christ is God. Therefore to try to drive a wedge between the righteousness of Christ and the righteousness of God is an unnecessary quibble. This righteousness credited or imputed to us is therefore 'the righteousness of God' (remember that phrase from Romans 3:21).

Think about the previous verse: 'We are ... Christ's ambassadors, as though God were making his appeal through us.' The very fact that Paul uses the names of 'Christ' and 'God' interchangeably in verse 20 means that we should have no such quibble about verse 21. We are Christ's ambassadors, so we might be expecting Paul to speak of

Christ making his appeal through us. But he doesn't. He speaks of it being as though God were making his appeal through us. God and Christ are one. The righteousness of Christ and the righteousness of God are one and the same thing here.

And what a gift to us this righteousness of God is! I think it will help us pastorally if we state what this is about both negatively and positively.

Negatively, this is to be contrasted with human righteousness. Remember what Jesus said in the Sermon on the Mount: 'For I tell you that unless your righteousness surpasses that of the Pharisees and the teachers of the law, you will certainly not enter the kingdom of heaven' (Matthew 5:20). On the surface this seems to be the most depressing verse in the Bible. Here Jesus is speaking about the Pharisees at their best, not their worst. He is not referring to the hypocrisy for which many of them were known, but to the honest zeal for the law which others of them had (see Romans 10:2-3). Many of these religious men could not have been more sincere and serious about trying to obey all God's laws and so attain to being righteous. But Jesus is saying that, no matter how hard you try, if you think you can be righteous by your own efforts, and so be acceptable to God, you will fail. You need a righteousness which is greater than the very best that human efforts can come up with — a righteousness greater than that of the scribes and Pharisees, a 'superhuman' righteousness. Doing your best will *never* be good enough. If this is true, where does it leave us? How, then, is there any hope? What you and I require is not a human righteousness, but a 'God-righteousness'. And that is precisely what is offered to you in Christ by faith.

That is what the ex-Pharisee Paul came to realize and rejoice in. He said that he considered all his strivings to merit a righteous status with God from his days as a Pharisee to be rubbish. Rather, his great hope since becoming a Christian was to 'be found in him, not having a righteousness

IMPUTED RIGHTEOUSNESS

of my own that comes from the law, but that which is through faith in Christ — the righteousness that comes from God and is by faith' (Philippians 3:9). To anyone reading this book who is relying on their good deeds or respectability, I have to say that it is time to realize the total inadequacy of such things. You need God's righteousness which is freely available by faith in Christ.

Positively, this is the 'righteousness of God' because it was wrought by the perfect life and obedience of God's Son, Jesus Christ. As such it is not simply provided by God, or approved by God, but it has a Godlike character about it. That is because it is Christ's righteousness, and Christ is God. Because this is so, not only does it meet all God's demands, but it always elicits his total approval. That is to say, not only does it warrant God's justifying us, but it guarantees that he will. Faith in Christ does not therefore just about scrape us over the demarcation line into heaven. We don't enter God's kingdom by the skin of our teeth. Rather, faith in Christ brings us the righteousness of God which flings wide open the gates of heaven and positively draws us into the kingdom. We are welcomed with open arms. It is 'the righteousness of God'. What a comfort! What a source of assurance! I sin; I fall; but as long as I have Christ, this is mine.

And it is this same imputed righteousness which also challenges us not to sin, but to live for God. It says, 'You are counted righteous in Christ, so start living out in practice what you are in status.' This is the whole dynamic of New Testament Christian ethics: 'Become what you in fact are. You are already clothed in the righteousness of Christ, so start living like Christ.' Again we will fill out this idea in a later chapter.

A question

We might have one last question about all this. Why does Paul speak in terms of our 'becoming', or 'being made', the righteousness of God in Christ? Why doesn't he use the word 'counted', as he did in verse 19?

There may be some mileage in the idea that Paul is looking forward to the completion of our salvation and therefore the fulfilment of all God's promises for his people — what he makes us to 'become'. In this case we, the redeemed, would be the proof to the onlooking universe of God's righteousness in keeping his covenant promises. In that sense we 'become the righteousness of God'. But it should be noted that part and parcel of God's covenant promises is the fact that he makes his people righteous in his sight (e.g. Isaiah 62:1; Romans 3:21). So to restrict the idea of 'the righteousness of God' to his covenant faithfulness even here cannot be the full story.

I think the great theologian John Murray puts the reason very well. He writes:

> The most significant thought of v. 21b is that we become this righteousness by union with him. We are not only made beneficiaries of it; we are made partakers of it and to such an extent that we are actually identified in terms of it. It is ours in the sense that our identity is defined in terms of it. Just as Christ became so identified with our sins, though knowing no sin, he was made sin, so we being in ourselves utterly ungodly and therefore knowing no righteousness are so identified with Christ's righteousness that we are made the righteousness of God.[1]

Paul speaks in terms of our 'becoming' the righteousness of God in order to emphasize how fully identified we are with Christ and all that is his. This all speaks to us of the rock-solid nature of our salvation. Those in Christ will never under any circumstances be rejected by God, for they are 'the righteousness of God'. What a salvation! The union between us and Christ is no tenuous link. Our righteousness is not a legal fiction. We are 'in Christ'. This is who we are. What a constant source of amazement, assurance and of adoration and praise to God!

Our being reconciled to God

Because we are clothed in Christ's righteousness we are fully acceptable to God. This passage is about reconciliation. Paul says, 'God was reconciling the world to himself in Christ, not counting men's sins against them. And he has committed to us the message of reconciliation' (v. 19).

In other words, God was acting so that he could forgive and accept sinners by the death of Christ and through the preaching of the apostolic gospel. Paul continues, 'We are therefore Christ's ambassadors, as though God were making his appeal through us. We implore you on Christ's behalf: Be reconciled to God' (v. 20). Then what we have been looking at in verse 21 is really Paul putting in a nutshell the substance of his gospel message of what God has done to make reconciliation possible: 'God made him who had no sin to be sin for us, so that in him we might become the righteousness of God' (v. 21).

Because this message effects reconciliation with God there are two things we need to do about it.

1. We need to believe it

We need to come to Christ and put our faith in him. If you are not yet a Christian, do not let your own perceived goodness hold you back — your goodness, as we have seen, will not be good enough. You need the righteousness of God.

Also do not let your sins keep you back, as though you were too bad to come to Christ. Look at verse 21 again: 'God made him who had no sin to be sin for us, so that in him we might become the righteousness of God.' Just as Christ's sinlessness was no bar to his receiving our sins, so our sinfulness is no bar to our receiving his righteousness. We might have thought that Christ's being sinless would make it impossible for our sin to be imputed to him, but it didn't. Similarly, we might think that our being sinners makes it impossible for us to have Christ's righteousness imputed to us, but it doesn't. It is no impairment to be a sinner, so come!

Also, I must add, do not let the thought of a deathbed conversion hold you back. Praise God, as we saw at the beginning of the chapter, because the gospel is what it is, holding the gift of imputed righteousness, there is hope even on the deathbed. But you don't know that there will be a deathbed for you, or whether you will have time to seek Christ then. Your end might be an instantaneous accident. You don't know whether you will even be here tomorrow. So, if as you read this you are not already a Christian, don't hold back. Come to Christ today.

2. We need to preach it

This is what we must do if we are Christians. Because this message effects reconciliation with God, if we already belong to Christ, we need to find every way and take every opportunity we can to share this wonderful news with our friends and family and whoever will listen to us. Paul says something in verse 20 which is true of every Christian: 'We are ... Christ's ambassadors.' Let's be those on the lookout and praying for opportunities to share the message. We have received this astonishing gift of imputed righteousness; let's tell others how they can receive it too.

What's the big deal for me?

The truth of imputed righteousness which we have considered here helps us to take in the fact that through Christ we can find full acceptance with God for ever, whoever we may be. This is a source of tremendous peace and security and can heal scarred lives.

Rebecca can clearly remember, as a child in Holland, her father attacking her mother, sometimes with a knife and often while drunk. Mother and the two girls would lock themselves in the bathroom while he pounded on the door in a rage. She can remember the police car coming to take them to a shelter for battered wives. After divorce, her mother came back to England with Rebecca and her sister, and they started attending church.

Rebecca says that at that time she pictured God as a benign, doddery old man and imagined that being a Christian was about helping God out. But she says, 'My arrogance was challenged at the age of seven when I went to a play about the Easter story. It was very moving to think about all Jesus suffered on the cross. Why should God have to die? At the end of the play I got a surprise. A woman in the row in front of me, whom I had never met before, turned around. She was a huge, smiling, black woman and she said, "Little girl, have you asked Jesus to forgive you all the bad things you've done?" I shook my head. "You must ask him to forgive you so you can go to heaven," she replied.'

Realizing that she was not such a great asset to God after all, on the way home in the car Rebecca curled up on the back seat and asked the Lord Jesus to forgive her.

Years passed and as she grew up Rebecca wondered whether Christianity really was true. She looked into other religions. She says, 'I did some research and was staggered to find that, whereas all other religions seemed to be about doing things to please God, Jesus only asks us to trust him and submit to his helping us. I found this so incredible because I had always worked hard to prove myself. I had once read a newspaper article suggesting that children from one-parent families were likely to turn to crime and do badly at school. I vowed to prove the article wrong. This had driven me. My life was about proving myself and trying to earn God's love. But I found instead that, through Jesus, God accepts us and gives us eternal life as a free gift. He is infinitely better than any earthly father. His love is unconditional.'

God's love is unconditional because Jesus has met all the conditions for us. Clothed in his righteousness, whatever our background, whatever the difficulties and deprivations we might have experienced, God accepts us in him. This is truly a cause for thankfulness and worship.

Big deal 5
Christ's obedience — all that God requires

ROMANS 5:12-19

Therefore, just as sin entered the world through one man, and death through sin, and in this way death came to all men, because all sinned — for before the law was given, sin was in the world. But sin is not taken into account when there is no law. Nevertheless, death reigned from the time of Adam to the time of Moses, even over those who did not sin by breaking a command, as did Adam, who was a pattern of the one to come.

But the gift is not like the trespass. For if the many died by the trespass of the one man, how much more did God's grace and the gift that came by the grace of the one man, Jesus Christ, overflow to the many! Again, the gift of God is not like the result of the one man's sin: The judgement followed one sin and brought condemnation, but the gift followed many trespasses and brought justification. For if, by the trespass of the one man, death reigned through that one man, how much more will those who receive God's abundant provision of grace and of the gift of righteousness reign in life through the one man, Jesus Christ.

Consequently, just as the result of one trespass was condemnation for all men, so also the result of one act of righteousness was justification that brings life for all men. For just as through the disobedience of the one man the many were made sinners, so also through the obedience of the one man the many will be made righteous.

> The law was added so that the trespass might increase. But where sin increased, grace increased all the more so that, just as sin reigned in death, so also grace might reign through righteousness to bring eternal life through Jesus Christ our Lord.

I HAVE been privileged, on a number of occasions, to speak at conferences of the pastors of the Africa Inland Church situated around Lake Victoria. On one of our early trips to rural Kenya I came across a little Kenyan boy for whom I was, I think, the first white man he had ever seen. In me he was confronted with something totally outside his young experience. He did not know what to make of me, whether to be frightened or to laugh. He stood looking at me and eventually he just fell over, causing his parents to smile.

There are some things which simply astonish us, take our breath away. For the Christian the truth that God justifies us, declares us and constitutes us righteous in his sight, even though of ourselves we are sinners, is one of those amazing facts. It is highly surprising — very hard to get our heads round. It is both scary and joyful at the same time, and when the penny drops with us that it really is true, it makes us fall down in love and worship.

Two kinds of obedience

Now a crucial aspect of the New Testament's doctrine of justification is commonly known as 'the active obedience of Christ'. This teaches that Jesus not only endured on our behalf the punishment of the law that we sinners deserved, but he also fulfilled the positive obligations of God's law on our behalf. His suffering tends to be called his 'passive obedience', and his positive keeping of God's requirements for a perfect life is referred to as his 'active obedience'.

God requires perfect obedience on the part of everyone who would attain eternal life, and Christ has provided this perfect obedience which we failing sinners could never attain for ourselves. Justification, therefore, includes two things. It consists of both the forgiveness of the believer's sins, based on Christ's passive obedience, and the crediting, or imputing, of Christ's righteousness, his active obedience, to the believer.

It is the part played by Christ's active obedience that we are going to look at in this chapter. We will do so via Romans 5:12-21. What follows is not a full exposition of that passage, but we will focus on what it tells us about Christ's obedience, especially verse 19: 'For just as through the disobedience of the one man the many were made sinners, so also through the obedience of the one man the many will be made righteous.'

There are two matters of central importance involved here:

- First, does God really require perfect obedience as the condition for eternal life?
- Secondly, does Jesus Christ provide this perfect obedience as the basis for our justification?

We will use those two questions as our main headings, and our investigation will, I trust, serve to underpin and illuminate further what we found in the last chapter concerning imputed righteousness.

So let's take up the first of those questions.

Does God require perfect obedience as the condition of eternal life?

This question is actually about the holy character of God. The Bible tells us that God is perfect and his perfect character will never allow the least infraction of his commands, or permit his justice to be compromised in any way. He is too pure to tolerate wrong, or even to contemplate evil (Habakkuk 1:13).

That is the kind of God he is. At the centre of his being is a glorious holiness which includes complete moral integrity.

In the second half of Romans 5 Paul sets up a comparison between Christ and Adam. We see God's requirement of perfection as we look at what our passage tells us about Adam's sin and its consequences. We are told, 'Sin entered the world through one man, and death through sin' (v. 12). Later in the chapter we read, 'By the trespass of the one man, death reigned through that one man' (v. 17). And in particular notice the first part of verse 18: 'The result of one trespass was condemnation for all men.'

To begin with we need, of course, to understand that Adam, the first man, acted as the representative, or federal head, of all mankind who would be descended from him. That is how his sin affected us all.

This concept of representation is not as unusual as it may at first sound. In a democracy we are all very used to electing politicians as our representatives. We elect them in the hope that they will represent our views and speak on our behalf. If, for example, they win the argument to keep the accident and emergency unit at our local hospital open, then we win; the whole town benefits. If they lose the argument, then we all lose.

Or think of the game of chess. The king is different from other pieces. Lose a bishop or lose a pawn, and the rest of the team can play on. But if the king is checkmated, the game is over for all the pieces. The whole team has lost.

That is how it was with Adam. He was a kind of king who acted as representative for all mankind. So when he fell into sin, there were consequences for the whole human race. We are told therefore, 'By the trespass of the one man, death reigned' (v. 17). Similarly verse 19 explains, '... through the disobedience of the one man the many were made sinners.'

Just one trespass

Now, as far as our question is concerned — does God require perfect obedience? — the verse to look at is verse 18. Here Paul tells us, 'the result of one trespass was condemnation for all men'. Just one trespass brought God's judgement. The demand for perfect obedience to God's law is already evident from the opening chapters of Genesis to which Paul is referring here. God made man in covenant with himself, requiring of him obedience, with the promise of eternal life for that obedience to his commands. The very first words God speaks to Adam and Eve in Genesis 1 are commands: 'Be fruitful and increase in number; fill the earth and subdue it. Rule ... over every living creature...' (Genesis 1:28). God commands the first human beings to act as his vicegerents to govern the earth and bring forth its full potential.

But previously in Eden, before the creation of Eve, God had given a specific command to Adam: 'You are free to eat from any tree in the garden; but you must not eat from the tree of the knowledge of good and evil, for when you eat of it you will surely die' (Genesis 2:16-17). This is law. Concerning Adam, in Romans 5 Paul speaks of him sinning 'by breaking a command' (v. 14). Also it is worth recognizing that the mode of expression, 'You shall not eat...', is the same way of speaking as in all the 'You shall not's of the Ten Commandments. So again this points to Adam's being a lawbreaker.

But what we must highlight from verse 18 as relevant to our question is, of course, that it was just one trespass that brought calamity on Adam and on us all. One act of disobedience brought tragedy. There was no second chance with God. There was nothing of, 'Well, this time I'll overlook what you have done, but next time...' That is because what God requires is not vague or approximate obedience. He requires (and deserves) perfect obedience.

Such a small thing?

God's command in Eden was not to eat the forbidden fruit (Genesis 2:17). I think the nature of this commandment of God — what we might loosely term the 'smallness' of the offence — indicates the same thing. It shows us that God requires perfect obedience. To modern ears the story sounds weird. To some extent we can understand why so many people dismiss the historicity of the incident and categorize it as mythical (though it is not). We can almost hear our secular contemporaries' outrage: 'All this judgement, and for what? The eating of a fruit! It's not even as if the sin was something serious like murder or rape, for goodness' sake!' But it is the seeming triviality of the offence that makes us sit up. It forces us to see that God really does require perfect obedience. If God has commanded something, however small, it is no longer trivial. The least missing of the mark is disastrous. We see again that it is perfect obedience which is required.

Just a scratch

All this might look ultra-pedantic on God's part. But that is to misunderstand what is going on here. Even at a human level, the smallest things which mar our prize possessions can be of enormous significance to us.

I was reminded of this recently when, while I was carrying a box of groceries for someone, I crossed the road between some parked vehicles and inadvertently scratched a neighbour's rather smart Audi car. It was just a small scratch, perhaps a couple of inches long. From a few feet away you could not even see it. I left a note for the owner on his windscreen admitting my guilt. Would he pass over such a small defect? No. His car was so precious to him that the whole panel had to be resprayed at a cost of several hundred pounds, with which I was charged.

Why did the man insist that his car should be resprayed and made to look perfect once more, without the slightest blemish? As you can imagine, I thought about this for a long time! Eventually I came to the conclusion it was because, as psychologists often say about men and their cars, his car said something about who he was, who he saw himself to be, his self-image. His car was bound up with his very identity. It symbolized the man himself. It was an extension of his ego. 'I'm a chap who drives a swish car like this!' was an important message to give as far as he was concerned. Any scratch or imperfection mattered to him. At one level there is nothing wrong with this. He had worked hard to earn the money to get that car. It was a special delight in his life. It epitomized his values and lifestyle. And for the car with which he was personally so bound up to be in any way damaged or blemished was something that tended to undermine or belittle him as a person and so irritated him deeply.

Now God's delight and his self-image are not in a car, but in something far more profound. They are to be found in his law. God is righteous and he delights in the law of righteousness, which is a deep and intense expression of his own character. It speaks of who God is. My point is simply that if human beings feel undermined and angered if, for example, their cars are damaged in any way, let's not misunderstand or misrepresent God for desiring that his law should be kept perfectly. This is not God being pedantic. An attack on God's law is an attack on God himself. It is an offence against who God is. Surely the eternal law of God is of inestimably more significance than that of a road vehicle which is going to rust away and become abandoned anyway in a few short years?

Is this still the case?

God really does require his commands to be kept perfectly. Is this still the case? After all, the world has changed since God's original creation. Sin has entered and taken root on Planet Earth. It has infected all humanity. What effect does the fall into sin have upon this obligation to perfect obedience? Has the bar been lowered to accommodate the new situation? Does God's requirement of perfect obedience remain?

Well yes, it does. It's still there. It's still there because God hasn't changed. The Lord Jesus underlines this, doesn't he? A teacher of the law comes to him and asks, 'What must I do to inherit eternal life?'

> 'What is written in the Law,' [Jesus] replied. 'How do you read it?'
> [The man] answered: 'Love the Lord your God with all your heart and with all your soul and with all your strength and with all your mind'; and, 'Love your neighbour as yourself.'
> 'You have answered correctly,' Jesus replied. 'Do this and you will live' (Luke 10:26-28).

God's requirement is for *all* our heart, not some of it; for *all* our mind, not the majority of it; for *all* our strength and *all* our soul. He still requires perfection.

Sadly, the problem is that, as sinners, we cannot perfectly keep the law; we cannot love him with all our hearts, or love our neighbour as we do ourselves. That is why we need God's mercy in Christ. And, of course, it is mercy which is the great theme of the parable of the Good Samaritan which Jesus went on to tell the teacher of the law who had asked the question about eternal life. We need God's mercy because if we approach him on the basis of law he requires perfection and we have no hope.

Is forgiveness enough?

In the Old Testament God instituted the animal sacrifices. These were prefigurements which pointed to the perfect sacrifice of the Lord Jesus for our forgiveness. As we think in this chapter about Christ's active obedience, we must not in any way lose sight of the absolute necessity of his passive obedience. Without this passive, suffering obedience, we would, of course, still be in our sins, condemned to eternal death. But the question is this: Is this passive obedience sufficient? Does forgiveness alone provide the right to eternal life?

An illustration may help us with this question. Imagine that a father tells his son to do his homework and promises him a trip to MacDonald's if he does it. The son fails to do his homework and receives a suitable punishment for his disobedience — loss of pocket money, or whatever it might be. May the son then, on the basis of his having been punished, claim the trip to MacDonald's? Justice must say, 'No, of course not.' He must still do his homework; the punishment for failing to do the task does not suddenly wipe out the obligation to perform it. The punishment does no more than put the son back in his original position, his past failure now dealt with.

The Bible teaches that the situation with the human race in Adam is similar. Even after the forgiveness of sins, there would still be an obligation to obey God perfectly. If the original promise of life to Adam was based on a probationary period of obedience, it seems strange to think that God would proceed to grant eternal life simply on the basis of man being forgiven for his sins and so returned to Adam's original state of guiltlessness. We see that something more is required.

This is not merely a logical debating point. One of the deepest problems with Old Testament Israel was that although they had the sacrifices to take away their guilt, they kept on being disobedient. Their attitude, based on the idea that forgiveness was enough, led to the problem being compounded. They fell into thinking that sacrifice would do in place of obedience. They thought they could do as they pleased so long as they offered the sacrifices to cover their sins.

'No!' shouted the prophets, 'God hates such an attitude!'

> Does the LORD delight in burnt offerings and sacrifices
>   as much as in obeying the voice of the LORD?
> To obey is better than sacrifice,
>   and to heed is better than the fat of rams
>   (1 Samuel 15:22).

So we conclude that not only do we need forgiveness, we need a positive righteousness as well. We require a perfect obedience to satisfy God's law. That brings us to our second big question.

Does Christ provide this perfect obedience as the basis of our justification?

The marvellous answer of the New Testament is 'Yes!' He provides us with the gift of righteousness, 'the righteousness of God', as we have seen it called in 2 Corinthians 5:21 and Romans 1:17; 3:21; 10:3.

The great hymn of the Moravian Christian Count Zinzendorf rejoices in this glorious gift as follows:

> Jesus, thy blood and righteousness
> My beauty are, my glorious dress;
> Midst flaming worlds, in these arrayed,
> With joy shall I lift up my head.

We are both forgiven and clothed in righteousness, and so we are fitted to stand before God himself.

And do not be misled. When Paul speaks of righteousness he is not using it as a kind of code word to signify covenant membership. He uses the word 'righteousness' with its natural meaning. He uses it in moral terms. For example, immediately after announcing that the righteousness of God is revealed in the gospel in Romans 1:16-17, he tells us why we need this righteousness. He writes, '[For] the wrath of God is being revealed from heaven against all the godlessness and wickedness [literally, "unrighteousness"] of men...' (v. 18). He clearly speaks of unrighteousness in moral terms as parallel with ungodliness. This is why the NIV translates the original word 'unrighteousness' in moral terms as 'wickedness'. Since 'unrighteousness' must be taken in moral terms, it indicates that 'righteousness' must be taken in moral terms too. Paul is clear that the righteousness of God is the answer to our great moral problem of sin and disobedience. It is the answer to our inability to be justified by our own righteousness.

The righteousness of God

What, then, is this righteousness of God, and how does it provide for our lack of righteousness?

As we follow through on Paul's comparison between Adam and Christ, this is explained in Romans 5:16-19:

> The judgement followed one sin and brought condemnation, but the gift followed many trespasses and brought justification. For if, by the trespass of the one man, death reigned through that one man, how much more will those who receive God's abundant provision of grace and of the gift of righteousness reign in life through the one man, Jesus Christ.
>
> Consequently, just as the result of one trespass was condemnation for all men, so also the result of one act of righteousness was justification that brings life for

all men. For just as through the disobedience of the one man the many were made sinners, so also through the obedience of the one man the many will be made righteous.

Here he speaks of the Christian's righteousness as the obedience of Christ. In the context of Romans 5, Christ is, of course, the 'Second' Adam and the representative, or federal head, of all who believe. Because that is the case, his obedience makes us who believe righteous in God's sight. Going back to that phrase we have pondered before, because we are 'in Christ' his obedience is counted ours.

Let's follow the logic of the verses. In verse 16 Paul states that the gift brought justification, in contrast to the condemnation which followed Adam's sin. Verse 17 explains what the gift mentioned in verse 16, which brings justification, involves. Those who reign in life through Christ are those who receive the gift of righteousness. Justification, then, entails receiving righteousness as a gift. Given all that Paul says elsewhere, this gift of righteousness must be the 'righteousness of God' in Christ, bestowed upon us.

Verses 18 and 19 confirm that we are on the right track. In verse 18 Paul says that justification comes through one act of righteousness. He then becomes most specific in verse 19: the righteous act by which we receive the gift of righteousness is none other than the obedience of the one man. The many are constituted righteous through the obedience of Christ.

Let's summarize: the gift brings justification (v. 16); this gift is the gift of righteousness (v. 17); this gift of righteousness focuses on one righteous act (v. 18); this righteous act is the obedience of the one man, Jesus Christ (v. 19). So in answer to our second question, 'Does Christ provide the perfect obedience as the basis of our justification?' Yes, he does!

CHRIST'S OBEDIENCE

TWO ISSUES

This is wonderful! But there are two issues related to all this that may be troubling some readers and that I want to clear up so that we are not left in any doubt about this joyful truth.

First, someone might ask, with verse 18 in mind, 'How can the obedience of Jesus Christ be spoken of by Paul as one act of righteousness? His life of obedience included many acts, didn't it?' I think the best way to answer this is to see Christ's life as obediently fulfilling one great command from God the Father — to glorify God in the salvation of sinners. This was the mission on which Jesus was sent by the Father. All that he did was directed to achieving that one great end, and so may legitimately be spoken of as one act of righteousness.

Secondly, worry might be expressed along these lines: 'Doesn't this emphasis on the obedience of Christ draw our attention away from the cross?' The answer is 'Absolutely not!' The cross was not simply atonement; it was the climax of Christ's obedience, the act of obedience for which all other acts of obedience were preparatory. Isn't that how Paul views the cross in Philippians 2:8?

> And being found in appearance as a man,
>   he humbled himself
>   and became obedient to death — even death on a
>   cross!

It is the pinnacle of obedience which sums up all his obedience. So never view this doctrine of the active obedience of Christ as in any way diverting us from the cross. And that being the case, I am sure — going back to our first issue here — that Paul does have the cross in mind when he speaks of 'one act of righteousness' in verse 18. It was Christ gathering up the summation of all that he was and had achieved and offering it in one great sacrifice for the glory of God.

The faith of the early church

This understanding, both that Christ takes our sins away and that we are clothed in the righteousness provided by Jesus' life of perfect obedience, is not something cooked up by the Reformers. As we have seen, it is there in the New Testament.

And we find that the early church believed it too. In his recent book *The Breeze of the Centuries*,[1] Michael Reeves quotes a work of apologetics known as the *Letter to Diognetus*. Dated somewhere between AD 150 and 190, its author is unknown and it may possibly have been addressed to the tutor to the emperor Marcus Aurelius. This is what we find written there:

> ... when our unrighteousness was fulfilled, and that it had been made perfectly clear that its wages — punishment and death — were to be expected ... he himself gave up his own Son as a ransom for us, the holy one for the lawless, the guiltless for the guilty, the just for the unjust, the incorruptible for the corruptible, the immortal for the mortal. For what else but his righteousness could have covered our sins? In whom was it possible for us, the lawless and ungodly, to be justified, except in the Son of God alone? O the sweet exchange, O the incomprehensible work of God, O the unexpected blessings, that the sinfulness of many should be hidden in one righteous person, while the righteousness of one should justify many sinners!

You can feel the joy and elation in the writer's words as he contemplates what God has done for us in Christ. Michael

Reeves comments, 'Reading the *Letter to Diognetus* is like reading Luther...'

APPLYING THIS TO OURSELVES

But this is not just theology! It is good news for all! Wonder of wonders that perfect, total, thorough obedience is counted ours by faith — and so eternal life is ours! So, with this great truth in mind, let's now make some applications to our lives.

Respectable non-Christians

First, do you see how this speaks once again to respectable non-believers who may be tempted to trust that their own goodness will make them acceptable to God? We have seen that God requires perfection. None of us is perfect, and we would be foolish to think that we are. We need the gift of God's righteousness which is the obedience of Christ counted as ours through faith in him.

Jesus told a parable of a man found improperly dressed at a king's wedding banquet which sounds shocking to modern ears:

> ... when the king came in to see the guests, he noticed a man there who was not wearing wedding clothes. 'Friend,' he asked, 'how did you get in here without wedding clothes?' The man was speechless.
> Then the king told the attendants, 'Tie him hand and foot, and throw him outside, into the darkness, where there will be weeping and gnashing of teeth' (Matthew 22:11-13).

It seems very unfair of the king to act in this way until we realize that it was the custom for great people like kings to offer wedding clothes to all who attended such a feast. It displayed their greatness to give such gifts.

In the Old Testament Zion is personified and speaks of the celebration of the Lord's favour:

> I delight greatly in the LORD;
>   my soul rejoices in my God.
> For he has clothed me with garments of salvation
>   and arrayed me in a robe of righteousness
>
> (Isa. 61:10).

At the eschatological wedding supper of the Lamb, we read of Christ's bride, 'Fine linen, bright and clean, was given her to wear' (Revelation 19:8).

It was not that the man at the king's wedding feast could not afford wedding clothes; it was that he had refused the wedding clothes that the king's servants had offered him. This is a stark warning that our own righteousness is woefully inadequate and that we should not refuse the righteousness offered to us through faith in Christ.

Assurance for Christians

Secondly, do you see how this wonderful truth of the obedience of Christ being counted ours once again brings assurance to Christians in the face of our sins?

As Christians, we don't want to sin as we used to, but we still fall into sin. Then we have this worry: 'Does that mean I'm no longer right with God?' But can you see now that your justification never at any time depended on your own righteousness, your own obedience? God has found a way to secure our salvation from the vicissitudes of our daily conduct. The perfect obedience of Christ is counted as your obedience, and whether or not you fall into sin is beside the point. Believers are right with God for ever because of the obedience of Christ.

Christ's Obedience

And so much is that the case that the very next question Paul has to deal with in Romans, so that people don't get the wrong impression, is 'What shall we say, then? Shall we go on sinning, so that grace may increase?' (Romans 6:1). Now he has an answer to that, which we will look at in our next chapter. But before we get to that I can tell you for certain what that answer is *not*. It is not, 'You must not go on in sin, or you will lose your justification.' Neither is it that your justification is incomplete and the deficiency must be made up by your own righteous acts. Christian believer, the righteousness of God is yours, and that cannot change. So be assured.

Just as if...?

Thirdly, do you see that the colloquial definition of justification that it's 'just as if I'd never sinned', although well-meaning, is a totally inadequate view of what God has done for us in Christ?

To be 'just as if I'd never sinned' would only be to put us back to what Adam was before the Fall — still on probation, still needing to provide our own perfect obedience. If that on its own were the gospel, it would not be good news. It would be leading us back into legalistic religion, having to meet God's demands, and never sure whether we had done enough. All joy in Christ would disappear. No. Christ not only obtained the forgiveness of our sins, he has given us perfect obedience. Christ has qualified us for eternal life.

And, if you think about it, even in heaven it won't be 'just as if I'd never sinned'. We will remember that we were sinners, and that will cause us to love and glorify God all the more! We will shout his praises: 'What grace to sinners!' 'Worthy is the Lamb who was slain!' The remembrance of what God has done in Christ for sinners will cause us to worship and adore for ever!

What's the big deal for me?

The Bible's teaching that Christ's obedience is counted as our righteousness sets us free from the Christian life becoming a straitjacket of religious duty.

Sarah's story brings the whole area of obedience into sharp focus. In her final year at university she had started attending a student Bible study and to her great surprise found that it made sense and was so up to date in what it had to say. Not having yet fully grasped the gospel, she decided to try to live as she thought a Christian should. When she moved to London she went to church and began attending a Christianity Explored course. I'll let her take up the story from there.

'I remember on week four or five of the course there was a question that asked, "If you were to die tonight and God asked you, 'Why should I let you into heaven?' what would you say?" There were a number of answers to choose from. One said, "You should let me in because I have read the Bible every day, because I have kept the Ten Commandments, because I have given money to charity and have generally been a good person." I remember thinking to myself, "Okay, Sarah, you can do this. You can be a Christian. It's going to be hard, but you can do it." But then I saw that this was the wrong answer! I saw that being a Christian was not about following a set of rules. The right answer is that God would only let me in because of what Jesus had done by dying on the cross to pay for my sins. This was the first time in my life that I understood there was nothing anyone could do to earn their way into heaven. This was the point when I became a Christian.'

Consequently Sarah began to seek to obey the Lord Jesus Christ. But this is what she says about that obedience: 'From then on, I continued to try to live a Christian life but my motivation was completely different. I knew that I was already saved and had a place in heaven because of Jesus' death. My new motivation was gratitude to Jesus.'

Religious people obey in order to try to be saved. Real Christians obey because *they have already been saved*. Jesus has done everything necessary. He has paid for our sins and perfectly served and glorified God on our behalf, and we are thankful.

Sarah underlines that new way of obedience. She says, 'God is not a killjoy who wants to ruin our fun. Rather, he is our Creator who knows what is best for us.'

Big deal 6
Sanctification — shall we go on sinning?

ROMANS 6:1-14

What shall we say, then? Shall we go on sinning, so that grace may increase? By no means! We died to sin; how can we live in it any longer? Or don't you know that all of us who were baptized into Christ Jesus were baptized into his death? We were therefore buried with him through baptism into death in order that, just as Christ was raised from the dead through the glory of the Father, we too may live a new life.

If we have been united with him like this in his death, we will certainly also be united with him in his resurrection. For we know that our old self was crucified with him so that the body of sin might be done away with, that we should no longer be slaves to sin — because anyone who has died has been freed from sin.

Now if we died with Christ, we believe that we will also live with him. For we know that since Christ was raised from the dead, he cannot die again; death no longer has mastery over him. The death he died, he died to sin once for all; but the life he lives, he lives to God.

In the same way, count yourselves dead to sin but alive to God in Christ Jesus. Therefore do not let sin reign in your mortal body so that you obey its evil desires. Do not offer the parts of your body to sin, as instruments of wickedness, but rather offer yourselves to God, as those who have been brought from death to life; and offer the parts of your body to him as instruments of righteousness. For sin shall not be your master, because you are not under law, but under grace.

THERE is a story that goes like this: a woman was walking down the street in a luxurious fur coat. An animal-rights activist approached her menacingly and asked through clenched teeth, 'Which unfortunate creature had to die in order for you to wear that?' The woman thought for a moment, smiled and then replied, 'Actually it was my mother-in-law'!

The Christian wears a far more wonderful garment — a robe of righteousness. This clothes us in such a way that we are fit to stand in God's presence. It totally exonerates us from our sins and positively commends us to God. It is a completely unearned, free gift to all who believe. It was at the cross that Jesus humbled himself to become a 'poor unfortunate "creature"' — the Lamb of God — who died in obedience to his Father's will to pay the price for our sin so that we might wear this robe of righteousness.

This is the joyous message of the gospel, explained in the first five chapters of Romans. There is 'a righteousness from God ... that is by faith'. This righteousness is more than a match for our sin. In fact Paul has coolly stated that the gospel of this gift of righteousness is so wonderful that God's grace is seen at its best where sin is at its worst: 'But where sin increased, grace increased all the more, so that, just as sin reigned in death, so also grace might reign through righteousness to bring eternal life through Jesus Christ our Lord' (Romans 5:20-21).

Now, with Paul prepared to make statements like that, we face a temptation. If we truly grasp what he has said, a question may easily arise in our hearts, sinners that we are: 'If I am not saved by being good, why should I bother to be good now that I am a Christian? If I am saved by faith alone, good behaviour cannot make me any more saved than I am already. In fact, since God's grace is seen best when sin is at its worst, why not go on sinning so that the grace of God might be more apparent?'

The freeness of God's grace in the gospel makes this such a live issue that Paul feels he must address it. It is the question posed in Romans 6:1: 'What shall we say, then? Shall we go on sinning, so that grace may increase?'

Today's church

This is not just a personal question for a Christian. It is also especially pertinent to today's church. Probably the most important question facing the church in the West for the last half-century has been whether, surrounded by a permissive, decadent culture, we are going to live holy lives? That question is still unanswered for many Christians and in many churches. There are numerous pressures on the church to compromise. The big shift that has taken place in Western society, and which we have already noted, is from a moral culture to a culture of emotion. 'Feel-good' is more or less all that matters now in our society. And, to many people, sin feels good. If we draw a line in the sand over any matter of Christian behaviour, almost immediately we are called 'judgemental'. Then others, in an echo of the sentiments expressed in Romans 6:1, would say that relaxing requirements for church membership, making the church more 'inclusive' — accepting easy divorce, casual sex, etc. — actually better reflects the love and grace of God.

In Romans 6 Paul takes up this issue of the need for Christians to live holy lives. His great insistence is that, though God's grace certainly *meets us* in our sin, it does not, and cannot, *leave us* in our sin. Though theologically you can talk about them separately, practically justification and sanctification cannot be divorced. They are joined in an indissoluble marriage. They always go together. Salvation must inevitably lead to a changed life, to godliness. Go on in a life of sin? Paul is absolutely appalled by the idea!

SANCTIFICATION

THE ANSWER IN A NUTSHELL

Why is that? In Romans 6:2 he puts his argument in a nutshell. Shall we go on in sin? Paul replies: 'By no means! We died to sin; how can we live in it any longer?' His summary argument is put in the form of a question so that the inherent contradiction and absurdity of such an idea will sink in.

'No one,' Paul is arguing, 'can be both dead and alive to the same thing at the same time.' You are either dead or alive; you can't be both! We don't believe in the 'living dead'. That is the stuff of horror fiction — not reality. 'A Christian,' says Paul, 'is someone who *has died to sin* — not simply someone who is *in the process of* dying to sin, but who has somehow *already* died to sin. Hence there is no way that a believer can ultimately pursue a life of sin.' It is impossible.

What does Paul mean? What is he getting at here? How are we to understand being dead to sin? The rest of verses 3-14 is an explanation and a proof of his statement in verse 2. We can follow Paul's argument under four headings. Walk with me through these verses.

CHRISTIAN BAPTISM PORTRAYS OUR UNION WITH CHRIST IN HIS DEATH AND RESURRECTION

Paul's argument begins with an appeal to Christian baptism. The assumption is that all believers have been baptized: 'Or don't you know that all of us who were baptized into Christ Jesus were baptized into his death?' (v. 3).

The most fundamental facts of the Christian faith are that the Lord Jesus Christ died on the cross, was buried and rose again. Baptism signifies our union with Jesus. We were 'baptized into Christ Jesus'. Baptism is a picture of our oneness with him in his death and resurrection. New Testament baptism was almost certainly by full immersion in water. Our going under the water portrays our death and burial (v. 3). Our coming up out of the water portrays our rising to new life: 'We were ... buried with him through baptism into death in order that, just as Christ was raised from the dead through the glory of the Father, we too may live a new life' (v. 4).

We have been joined to Jesus through faith (baptism is a concrete expression of that faith) and, now that we are joined to him, whatever is true of him is true of us. We are here once again being led to hark back to that wonderful phrase, 'in Christ'. We have become part of him, so whatever is true of him also relates to us. To use a simple illustration, my little finger is part of me. When I travel from Guildford to London, my little finger does that too because it is part of me. And since Christ died, then so have we died. And since Christ is risen, so are we risen. This is because we belong to him and are united to him. And the act of baptism portrays this union with Christ in his death and resurrection.

That is the first step in Paul's explanation of why we cannot go on pursuing a life of sin. Let's look at the next step. What else does Paul explain about this death and resurrection of Jesus?

Christ's death was a death to sin and his resurrection was a resurrection to God

Paul states clearly in verse 10: 'The death he died, he died to sin once for all; but the life he lives, he lives to God.' Christ's death included a death to sin, and his resurrection was a resurrection to God. We must probe this further. What is this death to sin Paul is talking about?

Obviously we need to understand this. It is a vital piece of the jigsaw. Three considerations will help to guide us.

1. *It cannot mean that Jesus died to 'indwelling sin'* because Jesus himself was sinless (Hebrews 4:15). Often

this passage in Romans 6 is misused to give poor Christians, weary with the battle with sin, the impression that there is some higher experience which can lift them out of the daily conflict. They are told that there is a higher plane on which they can live where there are no more struggles because indwelling sin will have been totally expelled from their hearts. But is that what Paul is talking of here? No, it can't be. Why not? Because Christ was sinless. He could not die to sin in that sense. So this passage cannot be talking about some immediate eradication of indwelling sin for Christians. Such an idea is a fantasy. We will know that higher plane of living; we will know total rest from the daily battle — but only in heaven.

2. So, putting that idea aside, we must move on. What is the death to sin Paul is talking about? Look at verse 7. It tells us that 'Anyone who has died has been freed from sin.' It teaches that *this death to sin is something that is common to all people who die.* This prompts us in the right direction. Anyone who has died, we might say, has departed from this world where sin holds sway.

3. But the real clue is in the context. Paul's statement in Romans 5:21 immediately precedes this chapter. He says, '... just as sin reigned in death, so also grace might reign in righteousness to bring eternal life through Jesus Christ our Lord.' There he is talking about the 'reign' of sin. We might say he is talking about the realm where sin is in control. It is in that context that Paul speaks about Jesus' death to sin.

When Jesus came into this world, he came into the realm where sin influences everything. This is a fallen world and under Satan's dominance. Jesus was not a sinner, but when he came into the world he entered sin's domain. He took upon himself a frail human body. He faced temptation, pain, weariness, Satan and death. But when he died — and here is the point — that relationship to the reign and realm of sin was ended.

Furthermore, since he had been gloriously victorious over all that the reign of sin had thrown at him while he was here on earth, he arose from the dead, showing that not only had he passed beyond sin's jurisdiction, but into a new sphere of glorious life in God. Christ was raised by the glory of the Father (v. 4) into a new life (vv. 4,10). He began his resurrection life. So this is the sense in which Jesus died to sin and rose again to God.

Let's link what we have learned back into Paul's argument. So far we have seen two things. First, we are one with Christ in his death and resurrection. Secondly, he died to the realm and reign of sin and is made alive to God. Our next step is this: we must put those two things together to get our third statement.

Through our union with Christ we too have died to sin and we too are alive to God

When did this happen? It happened when we were joined to Christ by faith, when we became Christians.

Jesus died to sin and rose again to God. When by God's grace we came to faith in Christ, his death and resurrection were actualized in us. What is true of him becomes true of us. So if you are a Christian it is not something that is going to happen to you, or ought to happen to you — spiritually *it has happened* to you. You have died to the realm and reign of sin. You no longer belong to this fallen world. Instead you belong to God's kingdom.

That is the import of verses 5-6: 'If we have been united with him ... in his death, we will certainly also be united with him in his resurrection.' Bodily resurrection hasn't happened to us yet, but all who are identified with Jesus in his death will certainly enjoy future resurrection through

SANCTIFICATION

Jesus too (v. 5) because Jesus is risen from the dead. We are destined for that resurrection world. In that sense we already, spiritually, belong to God's coming kingdom. This is the gospel.

But here comes the answer to the question with which we started. The ethical and spiritual implications of the fact that we died to the realm of sin and now belong to God's kingdom make impossible the idea of continuing to pursue sin as Christians: 'For we know that our old self was crucified with him so that the body of sin might be done away with, that we should no longer be slaves to sin' (v. 6). We belong to God's kingdom, where there will be no sin and we will be given resurrection bodies which are sinless and so enjoy the fulness of God's coming kingdom. Since this is our future, since this defines our true identity, sin has no claim on us. Sin has no part in who we now are. It is an anachronism in our lives which is to be discarded.

Changing nationality

Let me use an illustration to explain what I mean. Suppose a Frenchman changed his nationality and became British. Suppose he was then sent back to France to work for the British embassy in Paris.

Imagine the situation. Here he is in France, but he is not French any more. Here he is in France, but his loyalty is no longer to the French president — it is to the British Crown. Here he is in France, but French law no longer has any hold over him — he has diplomatic immunity.

It is the same with us who are Christians. Here we are still in this world, but we no longer belong to it. We died to it. We belong to another country. We belong to heaven; we are earmarked for the kingdom of God. Here we are where sin reigns, but sin is no longer our rightful master; the Lord God is. Its demands have no legitimacy over us. It is a 'law' which does not apply to us. Here we are in this world and sin still tries to allure us. But our hearts have been changed so that, though we still might feel temptation's pull and sometimes might even fall, our deepest loyalty is to Christ. We want to be faithful to him. Our old self has been crucified (v. 6), with the express purpose of doing away with sin in our lives and living the way of God's kingdom.

Further, since we died with Christ, we will certainly live with him (v. 8) in the resurrection. Now, since Christ died and was raised never to die again, so the Christian cannot go back to pursue a life of sin (v. 9). It makes no sense. It would be as inappropriate as it would be for Jesus, having won the victory over sin and death, to come back again and place himself once more under the jurisdiction of sin and death. No, having mastered sin once and for all (v. 10), to go back would be absurd.

So, 'Shall we go on sinning?' Shall we pursue a life that is based on this world, its values and its fallen desires? Paul's answer is a resounding, 'By no means!' Since all this is true, he now comes in with great encouragement.

SINCE ALL THIS IS TRUE, WE ARE TO LIVE A NEW LIFE

If the Christian church embraces the idea of 'continuing in sin that grace may increase', then it will become even more of a laughing stock than it is now. 'Christ can give you a new life,' we preach. But if the church embraces immorality, the world can rightly scoff and say, 'Don't be stupid. Just look at you!' It is imperative that Christians be different. And the good news of Romans 6 is not only that we *should* be different, but that we *can* be different. How? Paul spells that out in three short points in these verses of practical application.

SANCTIFICATION

How we see ourselves

First, if we are going to be different *we must recognize that we are different*. Romans 6:11 says, 'In the same way, count yourselves dead to sin but alive to God in Christ Jesus.' In the same way that we believe Jesus is alive from the dead, we must understand and believe that we belong to God's kingdom. Notice that it is not our counting ourselves dead to sin which makes our being dead to sin come true. It is the other way round. Because we *are* dead to sin, so we should believe it is so.

Let's go back to our Frenchman who has become a naturalized Englishman. We can imagine him one day walking through the streets of Paris. All seems just as it was before he became a British citizen. He might well be tempted to think that nothing has changed with him. His change of nationality might feel like an illusion: 'I am the same man, walking the same old streets, in the same old life.' But, no, he must not forget who he is. Similarly, we too must continually tell ourselves that we do not belong to this world. Why? Because God's Word says so. The Christian must learn to see himself or herself by faith. That is where our fight against sin must begin. The Frenchman may want something concrete to remind him. Perhaps he takes out his new passport, saying 'British citizen', and looks at it to recall who he really is. In just the same way, the Christian might want some concrete reminder. We can look back to our baptism, which was the outward expression of our faith. It took place at a specific location, at a particular point in time, in front of certain people as witnesses. So we recall who we really are. We belong to Christ.

Offering ourselves

Secondly, as a result of who we are, *we should resist sin and offer ourselves to God*. Pay attention to what Paul says next:

Therefore do not let sin reign in your mortal body so that you obey its evil desires. Do not offer the parts of your body to sin, as instruments of wickedness, but rather offer yourselves to God, as those who have been brought from death to life; and offer the parts of your body to him as instruments of righteousness (vv. 12-13).

Don't listen to Satan's lies which tell you that resistance is impossible. You can resist. You are a child of God! You have already been brought from death to life. You are not perfect yet, but you have been turned around. You don't belong to Satan's kingdom, so you don't need to do what he says.

Rather, we are consciously to present ourselves to God. We must make him the true object of our worship. We are to make ourselves available to him. We must consciously choose to place ourselves at the disposal of our Master and King. We make this choice in the light of the fact of who we now are. Because we belong to God, we offer ourselves to God for his glory and his good purposes.

There is probably a military image underlying what Paul says here. We are to choose to become weapons in God's hands for his war on Satan. In the great Old Testament incident of David's defeat of Goliath we are told that, having felled the giant with his slingshot, David took Goliath's sword to cut off his head. The weapon which Goliath had used to kill and plunder was now used to decapitate him. There is a lovely irony there. In the same way, we, who in our sinful state had been used by Satan to do wickedness, now have the wonderful opportunity to be used by God to do good. Having been so misused by the devil as to be on our way to hell, we now have the chance to get back at our brutal former master by becoming a weapon for good in God's hands. Think of all the ways Satan has deceived you and used you in the past to damage yourself and others.

SANCTIFICATION

Now instead make the daily choice to be a weapon of good for God, a weapon to thwart Satan's purposes.

Here is another illustration which might help us in following through on making ourselves available to God. We Christians are now like migratory birds. We have an inbuilt instinct for heaven. We are only truly happy if we are making progress towards it. That is why we must choose to resist. To follow sin is to put a ball and chain around the bird's leg. We cannot fly. We are frustrated. That is why the backsliding Christian is never at peace. Therefore 'offer yourselves to God, as those who have been brought from death to life'.

Freedom is coming

Thirdly, be encouraged in this pursuit of holiness because *you are not without resources*, and you will get there. Paul assures us with the following words: 'For sin shall not be your master, because you are not under law, but under grace' (v. 14). Sin shall not rule over you. That is a sure-fire promise. This is what Jesus purchased for us at the cross. God is at work in you, and no one is greater than our God.

We no longer have to merit our salvation. All the law can do is tell us what is right and condemn us when we fail to live up to it. It cannot help us. But we are not under law. We are under grace. We are part of God's kingdom, under his benevolence, under his saving power. We are under all the resources of God's redeeming and renewing mercy. Therefore, we can seek holiness with confidence that God will help us!

One of the most encouraging episodes in the Gospels concerns the fall and restoration of Simon Peter. You remember that on the night of Christ's betrayal he protested that he would always be true to Jesus and go with him even to prison and to death. He was full of good intentions. But the Lord Jesus knew him better than he knew himself. He said, 'Simon, Simon, Satan has asked to sift you as wheat. But I have prayed for you, Simon, that your faith may not fail. And when you have turned back, strengthen your brothers' (Luke 22:31-32).

Of course, sadly, Simon Peter did go on to deny Christ. But Christ did not treat him as he deserved. He dealt with Simon Peter in grace. He had prayed for him. And with the help of Christ's all-prevailing prayers, Simon Peter came through that terrible fall repentantly. He was restored to fellowship with Christ, filled with the Holy Spirit at Pentecost and went on to become a gracious, loving apostle, mightily used for God's kingdom. Not being under law, but under grace, he was mightily helped and transformed.

Even now, the New Testament tells us, Christ is praying for us. The help that Simon Peter knew, we shall know. 'He is able to save completely those who come to God through him, because he always lives to intercede for them' (Hebrews 7:25). God is at work. Christ's prayers will prevail. 'Sin shall not be your master.' This is all part and parcel of what Jesus purchased for us at the cross.

What's the big deal for me?

The exciting consequence of the Bible's teaching on sanctification which we have unfolded in this chapter is that our lives really can change for the better. We do not have to be locked into a regime of failure and bad habits. As Christians we are called to participate in the great adventure of becoming the people God would want us to be. Here a young man, whom I will not name, tells his real-life story of transformation in Christ:

'Before I was a Christian I welcomed a sexual fantasy world into my heart aged about thirteen. It lasted until I was eighteen when God met with me and turned me around.

'When I first tasted the waters of life, I repented of my sexual sin and had a new power in my life. I was assured that God would fix me, and that there was no darkness in my life to which he could not show himself superior. It was the death of Jesus in my place that provided this assurance.

'But as a young Christian I struggled, as many young men do, with living a pure life. I never went back to the preoccupation with sex of my pre-Christian days. I had weeks where my solid focus was on Christ. God gave me many opportunities to serve him. I saw a few people become Christians, one of the great joys in my life. However, what emerged was a monthly or two-monthly cycle. I would fall into temptation, be unable to resist and fall into sin.

'Outwardly, it perhaps looked like any guy's battle. I had accountability partners, and they consoled me in my struggles. However, I knew that things were getting worse, and I felt a sense of despair. Was I really just supposed to hobble on like this?

'My addiction was built on the following factors: denial that I really had a problem, an unwillingness to radically break with the sources of my temptation, ignorance that there were people with my level of problem whom God had changed, and living in a sex-saturated society which was a ready partner to my perversion.

'Where could a solution be found? Actually I had a worship problem. Key to the whole thing was the reality that life is not about offering my heart to the idol of sexual fantasy, but offering my worship to Jesus Christ, who alone satisfies the thirst of the heart. I give glory to him as the one who has set my heart free to live a new life, with and for him. He has washed away my defilement, and continues to lead me out of the pit of myself into honesty, relationship, accountability and service. He gave me the willingness to radically amputate all the sources of sin in my life: Internet, terrestrial TV, magazines, videos and DVD.

'It has not been easy. At times it has been painful. But for many years I have known real freedom. In Christ I have a new life that I never had before.'

To know that the transforming power of God is at work in our lives humbles us, and at the same time fills us with hope and joy.

Epilogue
Outside the city

CHRIST died outside the city of Jerusalem (Hebrews 13:12). Outside the city was also the garden tomb where the resurrection of our Lord took place (Matthew 28:11). It was from outside the city that he ascended into heaven (Acts 1:12).

Outside the city, therefore, we died and were raised with Christ. And the writer to the Hebrews takes up that theme:

> And so Jesus also suffered outside the city gate to make the people holy through his own blood. Let us, then, go to him outside the camp, bearing the disgrace he bore. For here we do not have an enduring city, but we are looking for the city that is to come (Hebrews 13:12-14).

He uses the theme to challenge us to live a new life outside the city — that is, resisting the influence of the prevailing cultures of the world. We are to be outsiders, following an alternative world-view and an alternative lifestyle from the mainstream — a lifestyle that the world rejects, but which is of heaven.

As we saw at the beginning of this book, the present 'city' of Western culture is in the process of throwing off a moral framework for life and replacing it with the culture of emotion where 'feel-good' holds sway. For the church this presents a tremendous challenge, because the whole understanding of the biblical gospel is predicated on a moral view of life in which sin really matters and being right with God takes precedence over feeling good.

The contemporary world

The classic evangelical doctrines of the cross, penal substitution, imputed righteousness and salvation by faith alone, are necessitated by the holiness of God and the moral principles which govern his universe. But these things, and the whole moral view of life they are based upon is now 'outside the city' for much of modern Western culture and much of the professing church.

As God's morality is set aside by the contemporary world and the hedonistic rule of 'feel-good' takes over, our society is both changing and suffering. As, for example, parents have set aside the necessity of teaching their children the difference between right and wrong and have placed far more importance upon building 'self-esteem', so that the youngsters might feel good about themselves, two things have begun to happen.

First, the 'feel-good' approach has turned many children and young people into addicts of various kinds. The American psychologist and philosopher of the late nineteenth and early twentieth centuries William James foresaw something of this. He once wrote, 'If merely "feeling good" could decide, drunkenness would be the supremely valid human experience.' And now we are surprised that we have a binge-drinking culture among many young people! Alcohol brings a feeling of well-being. On top of this, of course, there are drug problems and concerns about obesity, not only among children but across the population. Of course, if 'feel-good' is top priority then comfort-eating makes sense. The 'feel-good' philosophy produces addicts. Now obviously there is a sense in which we want children and young people to have confidence and to feel at ease with themselves. That is good and right. But if we set feeling good as being of greater importance than being good in a moral sense, and seeking right instead of wrong, then 'feel-good' knows few limits and the door is open to addiction.

Secondly, the 'feel-good' culture is producing a generation of aggressive narcissists. I am not saying that all young people are like this. But there is a definite trend in this direction among many which has been recognized by sociologists.[1] A poll held in 2006 asked children in Britain to name the very best thing in the world. The most popular answer was 'becoming famous'; second and third were 'good looks' and 'being rich' — God came last. Without God and without a moral framework, people in a 'feel-good' world worship themselves; they become narcissists. They see life as meaningless. They see nothing as ultimately worth living for except themselves and their own pleasures. They believe the world ought to revolve around them. And it turns them into ugly, vain, arrogant characters.

As we look at contemporary Western society, we see many things which seem not only evil, but irrationally so. We see youngsters hooked on celebrity culture. We see their constant desire for fame. And it makes them aggressive towards anyone who opposes them. We now live in the era of school and college shootings. Anyone who crosses them, they feel, deserves to die — literally. It makes them prepared to seek 'fame', or at least 'infamy', by videoing themselves doing such things and posting the pictures on the Internet. What is going on here?

We think of the case not long ago of a group of young people beating up a crippled boy and putting a video of the incident on Youtube for everyone to be shocked by it. There was a court case in Italy against Google executives for allowing this to be put on the web. But of course, it isn't the governors of the Internet who are to blame; ultimately it is the mentality of the young people who did such a thing which is the real culprit and the most worrying feature of what went on. What is happening to people, especially the rising generation? How can youngsters think like this?

The answer is that they are in the grip of the idol of self — self-love, self-admiration, grabbing the limelight in any way they can. The feel-good factor of the adrenalin rush that comes from being the centre of everyone's attention is what they live for. And, in an amoral world, who cares whether that attention is gained through being famous or being infamous, for doing 'good' or 'evil'? What does it matter? It feels good!

This is the world in which the Christian church is now being called to witness for Christ. To relinquish the truth that because we live in God's creation we live in a moral universe and to buy into the priority of 'feel-good' will be to fail our generation completely. We must stay with the Bible's teaching of moral absolutes based on the holy character of the living God. And because we must stay with that world-view we must stay also with the great evangelical doctrines that speak of the cross of Christ paying the price, dealing with the punishment our sins deserved and offering us righteousness before God as a gift through faith.

There is a deep spiritual battle going on in the West. Let me ask a question. Who is the most selfish, the most narcissistic being in the universe? The Bible would tell us it is Satan (1 Timothy 3:6; Matthew 4:8-9). Think about it. Just as salvation and the process of sanctification make Christians more like Christ and prepare us for heaven, can't you see that a whole generation is increasingly taking on the vain, arrogant character of Satan himself and, therefore, we must conclude, is being prepared for hell? That is the bottom line in the difference between a world-view of biblical morality and the culture which prioritizes emotion and feeling good about oneself.

Epilogue

The beginning and the end

The New Testament reminds us on its very first page that sin matters. In Matthew's Gospel chapter 1 we read of the birth of Christ, who was named Jesus 'because he will save his people from their sins' (Matthew 1:21). Sin, moral rebellion, really matters. It matters more than avoiding upsetting people.

Let's think about this statement for a moment. Ethnically 'his people' were the Jewish nation to which Jesus belonged. Reading this through twenty-first-century eyes would raise a few eyebrows. His people at that time were oppressed. Their land was occupied by the Roman oppressor. Modern attitudes would tell us that, yes, we might speak of the sins of the oppressors, but to speak of the sins of his own people when they were victims of the Roman jackboot is completely insensitive and inappropriate. The time of Jesus' birth was not the time to speak of saving his people from *their* sins. It would be most inappropriate. But the New Testament, though full of compassion for the oppressed, sees that, in this matter of moral failure before God, the issue is so great that it does not ultimately side with either the victim or the oppressor. It does not allow emotion to cloud the issue. 'All have sinned and fall short of the glory of God' (Romans 3:23).

Similarly, the New Testament ends with a tremendous notification that sin really matters. As the apostle John describes the new heavens and earth at the end of the book of Revelation, and invites all his readers to come to Christ and believe the gospel, he also issues a stark warning. With the city theme in his mind, he transmits the words of the glorified Lord Jesus to us:

> Blessed are those who wash their robes, that they may have the right to the tree of life and may go through the gates into the city. Outside are the dogs,

those who practise magic arts, the sexually immoral, the murderers, the idolaters and everyone who loves and practises falsehood (Revelation 22:14-15).

It is moral failure which shuts the door to heaven. Sin is serious and can only be washed away in the blood of Christ shed at the cross.

Holding on to the gospel in our times is not an easy thing to do. The New Testament warns that in the last times 'the man of lawlessness' will arise — and Western culture is turning away from law in the sense of universal morality. As this proceeds it will become increasingly hard to be faithful to the gospel.

But we must go outside the city on this and argue lovingly but firmly that God's law matters and sin matters, and it is because sin matters that the gospel must not be changed. We must remain true to the teachings of the apostles.

Notes

Introduction
1. Josephus, *Antiquities* 18:1:3; *Wars* 2:8:14; *Antiquities* 13:10:6; *Antiquities* 13:15:5. Quoted by David Bentley-Taylor, *Josephus: a unique witness*, Christian Focus, 1999, p.115.

Chapter 2 — Penal substitution
1. Alec Motyer, *The Prophecy of Isaiah*, IVP, 1993, p.429.
2. Donald Grey Barnhouse, *God's Remedy*, Pickering & Inglis, 1954, p.379.
3. K. Moody-Stuart, *Brownlow North: his life and work*, Banner of Truth, 1961, p.46.

Chapter 3 — Justification
1. Leon Morris, *Tyndale Commentary on Luke*, IVP, 1976, p.144.

Chapter 4 — Imputed righteousness
1. *Collected Writings of John Murray, Volume 2: Systematic Theology*, Banner of Truth, 1977, p.21.

Chapter 5 — Christ's obedience
1. Michael Reeves, *The Breeze of the Centuries*, IVP, 2010, pp.28-9

Epilogue
1. Jean Twenge and Keith Campbell, *The Narcissism Epidemic: Living in the Age of Entitlement*, Free Press (Simon & Schuster), 2009.

This book will repay careful study in Bible studies or for personal reading. It is an accessible introduction to the very important issues that it addresses. And it very helpfully sets out a clear, biblical, approach to the topic.

Josh Moody
Senior Pastor, College Church in Wheaton,
author of *No Other Gospel*

A clear, straightforward account of essential gospel truths, to counteract the dangers of unbiblical teaching. These are solid truths to live by — truly 'Big Deals' for each one of us.

Robert Strivens
Principal, London Theological Seminary

John Benton's *At the Cross* provides a gold mine of the riches of Christ for the taking. His writing style is crystal clear, refreshingly forthright, considerate to others, while compelling in its own biblical argumentation. The glories of the cross are put on display in ways that magnify Christ and lead the believer to new depths of understanding, humility and joy. In an age where confusion regarding the cross abounds, we may give praise to God for the biblical fidelity and profound simplicity with which Benton unfolds for us Christ's grace-filled and substitutionary atoning sacrifice.

Bruce A. Ware
Professor of Christian Theology
The Southern Baptist Theological Seminary Louisville,
Kentucky, USA

A wide range of Christian books is available from EP. If you would like a free catalogue please write to us or contact us by e-mail. Alternatively, you can view the whole catalogue online at our website.

EP Books
Faverdale North, Darlington, DL3 0PH, England

e-mail: sales@epbooks.org
web: www.epbooks.org

EP Books USA
P. O. Box 614, Carlisle, PA 17013, USA

e-mail: usasales@epbooks.org
web: www.epbooks.us

Sales of our books help to promote the missionary work of EP in making good Christian literature available at affordable prices in poorer countries of the world and training pastors and preachers to teach God's Word to others.